Cake Decorating at home

Cake Decorating at home

Discover the art of cake decorating for fun!

Zoe Clark

David and Charles
www.rucraft.co.uk

A DAVID & CHARLES BOOK
Copyright © David & Charles Limited 2010

David & Charles is an F+W Media Inc. company
4700 East Galbraith Road, Cincinnati, OH 45236

First published in the UK and US in 2010

Text and designs copyright © Zoe Clark 2010
Layout and photography copyright © David & Charles 2010

A catalogue record for this book is available from the British Library.

ISBN-13: 978-0-7153-3758-5 paperback
ISBN-10: 0-7153-3758-0 paperback

Printed in China by RR Donnelley
for David & Charles
Brunel House, Newton Abbot, Devon

Publisher Alison Myer
Acquisitions Editor Jennifer Fox-Proverbs
Assistant Editor Jeni Hennah
Project Editor Jo Richardson
Art Editor Charly Bailey
Photographers Sian Irvine
Production Controller Kelly Smith
Pre Press Jodie Culpin

David & Charles publish high quality books on a wide range of
subjects. For more great book ideas visit: www.rucraft.co.uk

Contents

Introduction

Welcome to my first book! I have been a cake designer for several years now. After making my own wedding cake in 2005, I fell in love with all aspects of baking and cake design, and then turned my passion into a profession.

I specialize in all areas of cake making and decorating, but here I wanted to concentrate on schemes for celebrations that can include the whole family in the creative processes. Having two children, I know how rewarding it is to get kids involved in baking and designing cakes. In fact, mine are now expert cookie cutters and cupcake decorators!

My style is simple, feminine and non-fussy, so with each chapter I have kept the designs and techniques relatively basic, as I wanted the book to appeal to the full range of skill levels. Some projects are harder than others, but I've kept these as straightforward as possible. All have easy-to-follow step-by-step instructions and accompanying photos, and I have included practical tips along the way to provide extra guidance and reassurance.

The book has 10 chapters, each focusing on a central theme with one main cake and 2 smaller, complementary designs, which can be made together or separately. All these cake concepts can be adapted to cater for personal colour or design preferences, or to suit a different theme or celebration, and I have offered suggestions for variations throughout. I've also included ideas for how you can extend the theme to your table decorations and décor, to create the perfect backdrop and atmosphere for the occasion. Let these inspire you and your family to make your celebratory event truly unique and memorable.

But the most important part of cake making and decorating is to enjoy it, so just get stuck in and have a go. Don't worry if your first attempts aren't perfect – you'll soon develop your own style and methods with a little practice. Good luck!

Baking essentials

◇ **Large electric mixer**
For making cakes, buttercream and royal icing

◇ **Kitchen scales** For weighing out ingredients

◇ **Measuring spoons**
For measuring small quantities

◇ **Mixing bowls**
For mixing ingredients

◇ **Spatulas** For mixing and gently folding together cake mixes

◇ **Cake tins** For baking cakes

◇ **Tartlet tins and/or muffin trays**
For baking cupcakes

◇ **Baking trays** For baking cookies

◇ **Wire racks** For cooling cakes and icing fondant fancies

General equipment

Greaseproof (wax) paper or baking parchment For lining tins and to use under icing during preparation

Clingfilm (plastic wrap) For covering icing to prevent drying out and wrapping cookie dough

Large non-stick board For rolling out icing on

Non-slip mat To put under the board so that it doesn't slip on the work surface

Large and small non-stick rolling pins For rolling out icing and marzipan

Large and small sharp knife For cutting and shaping icing

Large serrated knife For carving and sculpting cakes

Cake leveller For cutting even, level layers of sponge

Cake card Special card, thinner than a cake board, to which you can attach miniature cakes

Large and small palette knife For applying buttercream and ganache

Icing or marzipan spacers To give a guide to the thickness of icing and marzipan when rolling out

Icing smoothers For smoothing icing

Spirit level For checking that cakes are level when stacking them

Metal ruler For measuring different heights and lengths

Creative tools

- ✧ **Hollow plastic dowels** For assembling cakes
- ✧ **Turntable** For layering cakes
- ✧ **Double-sided tape** To attach ribbon around cakes, boards and pillars

- ✧ **Piping (pastry) bags** For royal icing decorations
- ✧ **Piping nozzles (tips)** For piping royal icing
- ✧ **Cocktail sticks (toothpicks) or cel sticks** For colouring and curling icing
- ✧ **Cellophane or acetate sheets** For run-out icing decorations, or for covering icing if you are interrupted while working to keep from drying out

- ✧ **Edible glue** For sticking icing to icing
- ✧ **Edible pens** For marking positioning guides
- ✧ **Needle scriber** For lightly scoring positioning guides and bursting bubbles in icing
- ✧ **Cake-top marking template** For finding/marking the centre of cakes and marking where dowels should be placed

- ✧ **Pastry brush** For brushing sugar syrup and apricot masking spread or strained jam (jelly) on to cakes
- ✧ **Fine paintbrushes** For gluing and painting
- ✧ **Dusting brushes** For brushing edible dust on to icing
- ✧ **Dipping fork** For dipping fondant fancies in fondant icing

- ✧ **Ball tool** For frilling or thinning the edge of flower paste
- ✧ **Foam pad** For softening and frilling flower paste

- ✧ **Frill cutters** For cutting borders and pretty edges
- ✧ **Blossom and star plunger cutters** For cutting blossoms and stars
- ✧ **Circle cutters** For cutting circles of various sizes
- ✧ **Shaped cutters** For cutting out shapes such as daisies, hearts, stars and wedding cakes
- ✧ **Five-petal rose cutters** For making large blossoms (see pages 78–83)
- ✧ **Moulds** Such as shell moulds (see pages 70–76) and lace moulds (see pages 94–100)
- ✧ **Thin plastic dowel** For forming streamers (see pages 62–67)

Basic techniques

Preparing cake tins

Before baking your cake, you need to line the bottom and sides of the cake tin to prevent your cake from sticking.

1 Grease the inside of the tin with a little melted butter or sunflower oil spray first to help the paper stick and sit securely in the tin without curling up.

2 For round cakes, to line the bottom, lay your tin on a piece of greaseproof (wax) paper or baking parchment and draw around it using an edible pen. Cut on the inside of the line so that the circle is a good fit inside the tin. Put to one side. Cut a long strip of greaseproof (wax) paper or baking parchment at least 9cm (3½in) wide, fold over one of the long sides about 1cm (³/₈in) and crease firmly, then open out. Cut slits from the edge nearest to the fold up to the fold 2.5cm (1in) apart. Put the strip around the inside of tin, with the fold tucked into the bottom corner of the tin, then add the base circle and smooth down.

3 For square cakes, lay a piece of greaseproof (wax) paper or baking parchment over the top of the tin and cut a square that overlaps the tin on each side by about 7.5cm (3in). Cut a slit at each end of the tin on two opposite sides. Push the paper inside the tin and fold in the flaps.

Layering, filling and preparing for covering

Preparing a cake for icing is one of the key processes in achieving a smooth and perfectly shaped cake. If the cutting, filling and coating of the cake is all done correctly, the end result will be a lot cleaner and free from any unevenness. Sponge cakes usually consist of two or three layers (see pages 34–39), but traditional fruit cakes are kept whole (see pages 40–41).

Materials

♦ Buttercream or ganache (see pages 42–43), for filling and covering ♦ Sugar syrup (see page 44), for brushing ♦ Jam or conserve (jelly or preserves), for filling (optional)

Equipment

✧ Cake leveller
✧ Large serrated knife
✧ Ruler
✧ Small, sharp paring knife (optional)

✧ Cake board, plus chopping board or large cake board if needed
✧ Turntable
✧ Palette knives
✧ Pastry brush

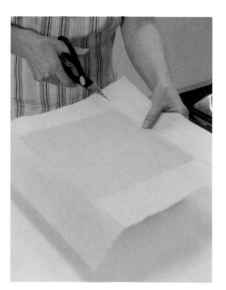

1 Cut the dark-baked crust from the base of your cakes. If you have two sponges of equal depths, use a cake leveller to cut them to the same height. If you have baked one-third of your cake mixture in one tin and two-thirds in the other, cut two layers from the deeper sponge with a large serrated knife or cake leveller so that you end up with three layers. Alternatively, you can cut three layers from a larger square cake, piecing together the third layer, as shown opposite. Your finished, prepared cake will be on a 1.25cm (½in) cake board, so the height of your sponge layers together should be about 9cm (3½in) deep. Use a ruler to check the depth. Most of the cakes in this book are this height, with a few exceptions.

2 You should have either baked your cake 2.5cm (1in) larger all round than required or baked a larger sponge (see pages 34–35). Cut around your cake board (this will be the size of your cake), cutting straight down without angling the knife inwards or outwards. For round cakes, use a small, sharp paring knife to do this and for square cakes use a large serrated one.

3 Once you have cut three layers of sponge, put them together to check that they are all even and level, trimming away any sponge if necessary. Place your base cake board on a turntable. If the board is smaller than the turntable, put a chopping board or another large cake board underneath. Use a non-slip mat if necessary.

4 Using a small palette knife, spread a small amount of buttercream or ganache on to the cake board and stick down your bottom layer of sponge. Brush some sugar syrup over the cake – how much will depend on how moist you would like your cake to be.

5 Evenly spread a layer of buttercream or ganache about 3mm (1/8in) thick over the sponge, then a thin layer of jam or conserve (jelly or preserves) if you are using any.

6 Repeat this procedure for the next layer. Finish by adding the top layer and brushing with more sugar syrup.

Tip

Make your filling thick enough so that the cake tastes moist and flavourful, but be careful not to add too much or it will sink when the icing goes on and ridges in the cake will appear.

7 Cover the sides of the cake in buttercream or ganache, then the top – you only need a very thin and even layer. If the coating becomes 'grainy' as it picks up crumbs from the cake, put it in the refrigerator to set for about 15 minutes and go over it again with a thin second coat. This undercoat is referred to as a 'crumb coat' and is often necessary for carved and sculpted cakes (see below), helping to seal the sponge.

8 Refrigerate your prepared cake for at least 1 hour so that it is firm before attempting to cover it with icing or marzipan; larger cakes will need a little longer.

Carving and sculpting cakes

It's much easier to carve and sculpt cakes when they are very firm or almost frozen, so chill, wrapped in clingfilm (plastic wrap), in the freezer beforehand. This technique is used in two of the main cake designs in the book, and specific instructions are given with these (see pages 70–75 and 86–91). When you come to carve or sculpt your cake, cut the sponge away little by little to prevent removing too much, especially if you are a beginner. Once you have achieved the desired shape, cover the cake with buttercream, or ganache if it's a chocolate cake, filling in any holes as you go (see above). Refrigerate until set and firm enough to cover with icing.

Covering with marzipan and sugar paste

Make sure that your cake is smoothly covered with buttercream or ganache before you ice it (see above), because if there are any irregularities or imperfections left, you will see them through the icing. You can cover cakes with a second coat of icing if necessary, or cover your cake with a layer of marzipan before you ice it with sugar paste.

Materials

◆ Marzipan (optional) ◆ Sugar paste
◆ Icing (confectioners') sugar, for dusting (optional)

Equipment

✧ Greaseproof (wax) paper or baking parchment
✧ Scissors
✧ Large non-stick rolling pin

✧ Large non-stick board with non-slip mat (optional)
✧ Icing and marzipan spacers
✧ Needle scriber
✧ Icing smoother
✧ Small, sharp knife

Round cakes

1 Cut a piece of greaseproof (wax) paper or baking parchment about 7.5cm (3in) larger all round than the cake, lay next to your work area and put your cake on top.

2 Knead your marzipan or sugar paste until it is soft. Roll it out with a large non-stick rolling pin on a large non-stick board, which usually won't need dusting with icing (confectioners' sugar), set over a non-stick mat. Otherwise, just use a work surface dusted with icing (confectioners') sugar. Use the spacers to give you the correct width – about 5mm ($^3/_{16}$in). Lift the sugar paste up with the rolling pin to release from the board and turn it a quarter turn before laying it back down to roll again. Try to keep it a round shape so that it will fit over your cake easily.

3 Pick the sugar paste up on your rolling pin and lay it over your cake. Quickly but carefully use your hands to smooth it around and down the side of the cake. Pull the sugar paste away from the side of the cake as you go until you reach the base. Try to push out any air bubbles that may occur or use a needle scriber to burst them carefully.

4 When the icing is on, use a smoother in a circular motion to go over the top of the cake. For the side of the cake, go around in forward circular movements, almost cutting the excess paste at the base. Trim the excess with a small, sharp knife and use the smoother to go round the cake one final time to make sure that it is perfectly smooth.

> ### Tip
> When working with icing, make sure that your work surface is free from any crumbs or other stray ingredients that can easily dirty the icing.

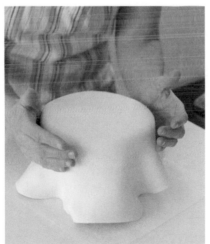

> ### Tip
> You need to work quite quickly with icing, as it will soon start to dry out and crack.

Square cakes

Square cakes are iced in a similar way to round cakes, but pay attention to the corners to ensure that the icing doesn't tear. Use your hands to carefully cup the icing around the corners before you start working it down the sides. Mend any tears with clean soft icing as soon as possible so that the icing blends together well.

Shaped cakes

For shaped cakes, you will need to use your hands more to act as the smoothing tool. Make sure they are not too hot! There are also various shaped smoothers available that you may find helpful to allow you to get into small ridges and tackle concave surfaces.

> ### Tip
> Gather up any leftover icing immediately and keep it well wrapped in a plastic bag to prevent it from drying out.

Icing cake boards

Covering the base cake board with icing makes a huge difference to the finished cake, giving it a clean, professional finish. By carefully choosing the right colour for the icing, the board can be incorporated into the design of the cake itself.

Moisten the board with some water. Roll out the sugar paste to 4mm (a generous ⅛in), ideally using icing or marzipan spacers. Pick the icing up on the rolling pin and lay it over the cake board. Place the board either on a turntable or bring it towards the edge of the work surface so that the icing is hanging down over it. Use your icing smoother in a downwards motion to cut a smooth edge around the board. Cut away any excess. Finish by smoothing the top using circular movements to achieve a flat and perfectly smooth surface for your cake to sit on. Leave to dry overnight.

How much marzipan and/or sugar paste you need

This chart gives an estimate of the quantities you will need to cover different-sized cakes and cake boards; square cakes will require slightly more than round cakes. If you are not very experienced at covering cakes, allow a bit extra than specified here. These quantities are based on cakes about 9cm (3½in) deep.

Cake size	10cm (4in)	13cm (5in)	15.5cm (6in)	18cm (7in)	20cm (8in)	23cm (9in)	25.5cm (10in)
Covering cake (marzipan /sugar paste)	400g (14oz)	500g (1lb 2oz)	650g (1lb 7oz)	750g (1lb 10oz)	850g (1lb 14oz)	1kg (2lb 4oz)	1.25kg (2lb 12oz)
Icing cake board	300g (10½oz)	350g (12oz)	425g (15oz)	550g (1lb 4oz)	625g (1lb 6oz)		

Securing ribbon around cake boards

To finish your cake off in style, attach some double-faced satin ribbon around the board to coordinate with the cake design and colour scheme. I use 1.5cm- (⅝in-) wide ribbon for this. Stick the ribbon in place with double-sided tape at intervals around the board.

> **Tip**
> For square cakes, put the double-sided tape around each corner, as well as a small piece in the centre of each side.

Assembling tiered cakes

Stacking cakes on top of one another is not a difficult process, but it needs to be done in the right way so that you can rest assured that the cake is structurally sound. I prefer to use hollow plastic dowels, as they are very sturdy and easily cut to the correct height. Thinner plastic dowels can be used for smaller cakes. As a general guide, use three dowels for a round cake and four for square. Use more dowels for larger cakes.

1 Use the cake-top marking template to find the centre of your base cake.

2 Using a needle scriber or marking tool, mark the cake where the dowels should go. These need to be positioned well inside the diameter of the cake to be stacked on top.

3 Push a dowel into the cake where it has been marked. Using an edible pen, mark the dowel where it meets the top of the cake.

Materials

♦ Stiff royal icing (see page 29)
♦ Iced cake board (see page 16)

Equipment

✧ Cake-top marking template
✧ Needle scriber or marking tool
✧ Hollow plastic dowels
✧ Edible pen
✧ Large serrated knife
✧ Spare cake board
✧ Spirit level
✧ Icing smoothers

Tip

If your cake is slightly uneven, push the dowel into the tallest part of the cake.

4 Remove the dowel and cut it at the mark with a serrated knife. Cut the other dowels to the same height and insert them all into the cake. Place a cake board on top of the dowels and check that they are equal in height by using a spirit level on the board.

5 Stick your base cake on to the centre of your iced cake board with some stiff royal icing. Use your smoothers to move it into position if necessary. Allow the icing to set for a few minutes before stacking on the next tier. Repeat to attach a third tier, if using.

> **Tip**
>
> Wait a couple of minutes before moving the assembled cakes so that the icing has had time to set a bit.

Cake stands

Tiered cake stands are a great way to display cupcakes and other miniature cakes. Homemade stands can be tailor made to suit your occasion, in any size and shape you want, by adapting the following basic method. Use any width of wide ribbon to wind around the centre column.

Materials

♦ 18cm (7in) and 10cm (4in) cake dummies, 10cm (4in) deep ♦ 33cm (13in), 25.5cm (10in) and 18cm (7in) iced cake boards (see page 16)
♦ Stiff royal icing (see page 29)

Equipment

✧ Icing smoothers
✧ Icing smoothers
✧ Wide ribbon
✧ 1.5cm (⅝in) ribbon
✧ Double-sided tape
✧ Scissors

1 Secure the largest cake dummy to the largest iced cake board in the centre with stiff royal icing. Repeat this with the smaller dummy and next size of board. The smallest board will not have a dummy!

2 Wind your wide ribbon around the centre pillar until it is completely covered. Trim and secure with double-sided tape. Cut another strip of ribbon slightly longer than the depth of the cake to cover the join. Attach the 1.5cm-(⅝in-) wide ribbon around the edge of the cake boards with more pieces of tape. Stack the tiers up and if you wish secure in place with some royal icing, making sure that your stand is level as you go.

Miniature cakes

These cakes are cut from larger pieces of cake (see pages 34–39) and are layered, filled and iced in a similar fashion to the larger cakes. Bake a square cake and cut your cakes from this, either round or square. The size of the cake will depend on how many cakes you require and the size you would like them to be. Always choose a slightly larger size of cake than you need to allow for wastage. For nine 5cm (2in) square mini cakes (I usually make them this size), you would need an 18cm (7in) square cake. Use only two-thirds of the quantities of ingredients in the charts, as mini cakes are not as deep as large cakes. Bake all the mixture in one tin rather than dividing it between two for larger cakes.

> **Tip**
> You could also make mini traditional fruit cakes (see pages 40–41), but the mixture would need to be baked in small, individual tins, as they can't be cut out due to their structure.

Materials

♦ Large square baked classic sponge cake, classic chocolate cake or white chocolate cake (see pages 34–39) ♦ Sugar syrup (see page 44) ♦ Buttercream or ganache (see pages 42–43) ♦ Sugar paste

Equipment

✧ Cake leveller
✧ Circle cutter or serrated knife
✧ Pastry brush
✧ Cake card (optional)
✧ Palette knife
✧ Large non-stick rolling pin
✧ Large non-stick board with non-slip mat
✧ Metal ruler
✧ Large, sharp knife
✧ Large circle cutter or small, sharp knife
✧ 2 icing smoothers

1 Slice your large square cake horizontally into two even layers using a cake leveller. Cut small individual rounds (using a cutter) or squares (using a serrated knife).

2 Brush the pieces of sponge with sugar syrup and sandwich together with either buttercream, or ganache if using a chocolate-flavoured cake. It is easier if you stick the bottom piece of cake to a cake card the same size and shape as your mini cake, using buttercream or ganache, but not essential. Working quickly, pick up each cake and cover the sides evenly with buttercream or ganache. Finish by covering the top and then place the cakes in the refrigerator for at least 20 minutes to firm up.

> **Tip**
> It's much easier to work with the sponge if it's very cold, as it will be a good deal firmer.

3 Roll out a piece of sugar paste 38cm (15in) square and 5mm (³/₁₆in) thick with a large non-stick rolling pin on a large non-stick board set over a non-slip mat. Cut 9 small squares and lay one over each cake. If you are a beginner, do half the cakes at a time, keeping the other squares under clingfilm (plastic wrap) to prevent them drying out.

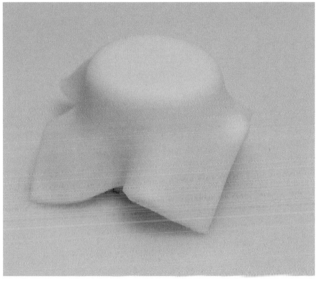

4 Use your hands to work the icing down around the sides of the cake and trim away the excess with a large circle cutter or small, sharp knife.

5 Use two icing smoothers on either side of the cake going forwards and backwards and turning the cake as you go to create a perfectly smooth result. Leave the icing to dry, ideally overnight, before decorating the cakes.

Baking cupcakes

Cupcakes are made in exactly the same way as the classic sponge cake, classic chocolate cake or white chocolate cake (see pages 34–39). The amount of ingredients you need will depend on the size of your cases. For 10–12 cupcakes, use the quantities given for a 13cm (5in) round or 10cm (4in) square cake. Use cupcakes cases (liners) to bake the mixture, placing them in tartlet tins or muffin trays and filling two-thirds to three-quarters full. Bake in a preheated oven at 180°C/350°F/Gas Mark 4 for about 20 minutes until springy to the touch.

Cupcake cases (liners) come in plain or patterned paper, or in foil in a range of colours. I prefer to use plain foil ones, as they keep the cakes fresh and don't detract from the decoration on the cakes. But you can use decorative cases (liners) for plainer cupcakes.

Cupcakes can be iced in various ways, depending on the look and taste you want to achieve. While some techniques are more involved and a little tricky to accomplish, others are much simpler and are great way to get the children involved.

Decorating cupcakes with buttercream

This is the simplest way to decorate cupcakes. You can pipe the buttercream on using a large plastic piping (pastry) bag fitted with either a plain or star-shaped nozzle (tip), which will take a little practice to get each cake looking perfect. Alternatively, simply use a palette knife to spread the buttercream on evenly to create an attractive domed top.

Tip
You may need to re-beat your buttercream to ensure that it's soft when you use it.

Fondant-dipped cupcakes

This way of decorating cupcakes is much more involved, but liquid fondant really makes a delicious and lovely looking little cake. I have used ready-made fondant here, which you can buy from specialist suppliers, but you can use a powdered fondant instead, available from most good supermarkets.

1 Prepare the cupcakes by shaving off any uneven bumps with a small, sharp serrated knife so that they are perfectly shaped, keeping them in their cases (liners). Brush the tops with the flavoured sugar syrup.

2 Bring the apricot masking spread or strained jam (jelly) to the boil in a saucepan and leave to cool slightly before brushing over the cupcakes with a pastry brush. Refrigerate the cakes for at least 15–30 minutes while you prepare the fondant.

3 Put the fondant in a microwave-proof bowl and warm in the microwave for about 1½ minutes on medium power until it can be easily poured from the bowl.

4 Add the glucose and three-quarters of the unflavoured sugar syrup and gently stir together, trying to avoid introducing too many air bubbles. Add any colouring. If you are dipping cakes in more than one colour, split the fondant between two or more bowls beforehand. Cover the bowl or bowls you are not using immediately with clingfilm (plastic wrap).

5 Return the fondant to the microwave and heat it gently until slightly warmer than body temperature (39–40°C/102–104°F), but no hotter. Test the consistency by dipping one of the cupcakes into the fondant. If it's too thick, add the remaining unflavoured sugar syrup until the fondant coats the cupcake well. Be careful not make it too runny or the fondant won't set.

6 Dip the tops of the cupcakes one at a time in the fondant, holding the cake by its case (liner). Allow the excess to drip down for a second and turn it back up the right way to set. Once you have dipped all the cupcakes, you may need to give them a second coating; wait 5–10 minutes for the first coat to dry before doing so.

Materials Makes 20

♦ 20 domed-shaped cupcakes (see opposite)
♦ 1 quantity sugar syrup, flavoured to match the sponge, and 1 quantity unflavoured (see page 44) ♦ 100g (3½oz) apricot masking spread or strained jam (jelly) ♦ 1kg (2lb 4oz) tub ready-made fondant ♦ 1 tablespoon liquid glucose ♦ Food colouring, as required

Equipment

✧ Small, sharp serrated knife
✧ Pastry brush
✧ Microwave oven and microwave-proof bowl
✧ 2 metal spoons or palette knife

Fondant fancies

These are a great alternative to cupcakes. Like the miniature cakes (see pages 20–21), they are cut from a square or rectangular classic sponge cake (see pages 34–35) and can be a variety of shapes, although the easiest to make are square. If they are to fit in a cupcake case (liner), they should be about 4cm (1½in) square and 4cm (1½in) high. Bake shallow cakes (see Materials right) and trim the top and bottom to give you the correct height. Vanilla, lemon or orange-flavoured sponge works best for fondant fancies.

The fondant icing is prepared in exactly the same way as for the cupcakes (see page 23), but the technique used when dipping them is quite different.

1 Once you have layered, filled and stuck the sponge back together, brush the remaining flavoured sugar syrup over the top of the sponge before covering it with a thin layer of the apricot masking spread or jam (jelly).

2 Roll the marzipan or sugar paste out with a large non-stick rolling pin on a large non-stick board set over a non-slip mat to 3–4mm (⅛in) thick, using the spacers to guide you. Lay it over your sponge and run the smoother over the top so that it is firmly stuck down. Mark and cut 4cm (1½in) squares with a sharp knife, keeping the squares together until you are ready to dip them. Place the sponge in the refrigerator and chill for at least 1 hour.

Materials Makes 16

♦ 18cm (7in) square shallow classic sponge cake (see pages 34–35, but use half the quantities specified), split into two layers and filled with jam (jelly), marmalade or lemon, lime or orange curd (see pages 12–13) ♦ 1 quantity sugar syrup, flavoured to match the sponge, and 1 quantity unflavoured (see page 44) ♦ 2 tablespoons apricot masking spread or strained jam (jelly), boiled and slightly cooled ♦ 175g (6oz) marzipan or sugar paste ♦ 750g (1lb 10oz) ready-made fondant ♦ ¾ tablespoon liquid glucose ♦ Food colouring, as required

Equipment

✧ Pastry brush
✧ Large non-stick rolling pin
✧ Large non-stick board with non-slip mat
✧ Icing or marzipan spacers
✧ Icing smoothers
✧ Metal ruler
✧ Large, sharp knife
✧ Dipping fork
✧ Wire rack
✧ Small, sharp knife
✧ 16 cupcake cases (liners)

3 Prepare the fondant by following Steps 3–5 on page 23 for Fondant-dipped Cupcakes, using the unflavoured sugar syrup.

4 Cut away any excess trimmings from the sponge. Plunge each square fancy, marzipan/icing side down, into your warm fondant. Working quickly, use the dipping fork to turn the fancy back upwards and move it across to the wire rack to allow the excess icing to drip down and off the sides of the cake. Repeat for each fancy.

5 Remove the fancies from the rack using a small, sharp knife to cut away any excess fondant.

6 Place each fancy into a cupcake case (liner) that has been slightly pressed out beforehand so that the cake fits easily inside. Cup the case (liner) back up around the sides of the cake so that it takes on its shape. Place the fancies together, side by side, until they are completely set and ready to decorate.

Baking cookies

Cookies are great fun to make – ideal for getting children involved – and are suitable for just about any occasion. You can cut out any shapes from the cookie dough and decorate them however you like. In this book, you will learn how to use a variety of techniques to create eye-catching and delicious treats that are sure to impress.

This dough can be made up to two weeks ahead or stored in the freezer until ready to use.

Materials

Makes 10–15 large or 25–30 medium

♦ 250g (9oz) unsalted butter ♦ 250g (9oz) caster (superfine) sugar ♦ 1–2 medium eggs ♦ 1 teaspoon vanilla extract ♦ 500g (1lb 2oz) plain (all-purpose) flour, plus extra for dusting

Equipment

✧ Large electric mixer
✧ Spatula
✧ Deep tray or plastic container
✧ Clingfilm (plastic wrap)
✧ Rolling pin
✧ Cookie cutters or templates
✧ Sharp knife (if using templates)
✧ Baking trays
✧ Greaseproof (wax) paper or baking parchment

1 In a bowl of an electric mixer, beat the butter and sugar together until creamy and quite fluffy.

2 Add the eggs and vanilla extract and mix until they are well combined.

3 Sift the flour, add to the bowl and mix until all the ingredients just come together. You may need to do this in two stages – do not over-mix.

4 Tip the dough into a container lined with clingfilm (plastic wrap) and press down firmly. Cover with clingfilm (plastic wrap) and refrigerate for at least 30 minutes.

5 On a work surface lightly dusted with flour, roll out the cookie dough to about 4mm (⅛in) thick. Sprinkle a little extra flour on top of the dough as you roll to prevent it from sticking to the rolling pin.

> ### Tip
> Be careful not too add too much flour when you are rolling out your dough, as it will become too dry.

6 Cut out your shapes either with cutters or using templates and a sharp knife. Place on baking trays lined with greaseproof (wax) paper or baking parchment and return to the refrigerator to rest for at least 30 minutes.

7 Bake the cookies in a preheated oven at 180°C/350°F/Gas Mark 4 for about 10 minutes, depending on their size, or until they are golden brown. Leave them to cool completely before storing them in an airtight container until you are ready to decorate them. The baked cookies will keep for up to one month.

Flavour variations

Chocolate Substitute 50g (1¾oz) flour with cocoa powder (unsweetened cocoa).

Citrus Add the finely grated zest of 1 lemon or orange.

Almond Replace the vanilla extract with 1 teaspoon almond extract.

Covering cookies with sugar paste

This a very simple and quick way to ice cookies, yet still looks really neat and effective. Roll out some sugar paste to no more than 4mm (⅛in) thick and cut out the shape of the cookie using the same cutter or template used for the cookie dough. Stick the icing on to the cookie using boiled and cooled apricot masking spread or strained jam (jelly), taking care not to stretch it out of shape.

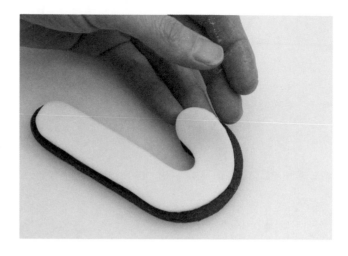

Royal-iced cookies

This is my favourite method of icing cookies, as I love the taste of the crisp white icing against the softer texture of the cookie underneath. Most of the cookie projects in this book have been iced this way.

1 Place the No. 1.5 nozzle (tip) in a small piping (pastry) bag and fill with some soft-peak royal icing. Pipe an outline around the edge of each cookie.

2 Thin down some more royal icing with water until 'flooding' consistency (see opposite) and place in large piping (pastry) bag fitted with the No. 1 nozzle (tip). Use to flood inside the outlines on the cookies with icing. For larger cookies or 'run-outs' (see opposite), you can snip off the tip of the bag instead of using a nozzle (tip).

3 Once dry, pipe over any details that are required and stick on any decorations.

Materials

♦ Soft-peak royal icing (see opposite)

Equipment

✧ Paper piping (pastry) bags, small and large (see page 30)
✧ Piping nozzles (tips): No. 1.5 and No. 1 plain

> ### Tip
> If you are icing lots of cookies, use a squeezable plastic bottle with a small nozzle (tip) instead of piping (pastry) bags.

> ### Tip
> If the area you need to 'flood' is relatively large, work round the edges of the piped outline and then work inwards to the centre to ensure an even covering.

Royal icing

Working with royal icing is one of the most useful skills to learn in cake decorating. It is a highly versatile medium, as it can be used for icing cakes and cookies, for intricate piping of decorations (borders, flowers and lettering) or for simply attaching and sticking.

The icing is best used as fresh as possible, but it will keep for up to five days in an airtight container. Re-beat the mixture back to its correct consistency before use if it is not used immediately.

1 If using dried egg powder, soak the powder in the water for at least 30 minutes in advance, but ideally overnight in the refrigerator.

2 Sift the icing (confectioners') sugar into the mixing bowl of an electric mixer and add the egg whites or strained reconstituted egg mixture.

Soft-peak royal icing

In order to pipe various patterns and decorations easily, you may need to add a tiny amount of water to your royal icing so that the consistency is a bit softer.

'Run-out' icing

Royal icing is thinned down with more water to make 'run-outs' (smooth iced decorations – see Step 1, page 104), as well as to 'flood' (fill in) cookies (see opposite). For the desired consistency, test the icing by lifting your spoon and letting the icing drip back into the bowl. The icing falling back into the bowl should remain on the surface for five seconds before disappearing. If it is too runny it will run over the outlines and sides of the cookies, but if it is too stiff it won't spread very well.

'Run-outs' are done on a cellophane or acetate sheet, which is greased with a little white vegetable fat (shortening) and then placed, greased side up, over a template. Pipe around the outline of the shape and then 'flood' with icing, in the same way as for royal-iced cookies (see opposite).

Materials

♦ 2 medium egg whites or 15g (½oz) dried egg albumen powder mixed with 75ml (2½fl oz) water
♦ 500g (1lb 2oz) icing (confectioners') sugar

Equipment

✧ Large electric mixer
✧ Sieve (strainer)
✧ Spatula

3 Mix together on a low speed for about 3–4 minutes until the icing has reached a stiff-peak consistency, which is what you need for sticking on decorations and gluing cakes together.

4 Store the icing in an airtight container covered with a damp, clean cloth to prevent it from drying out.

Drop-in flooding

This technique is when you 'drop' a different-coloured, runny icing into the flooding icing when it is still wet which gives a slightly different, more blended effect.

Making a piping (pastry) bag

1 Cut two equal triangles from a large square of greaseproof (wax) paper or baking parchment. As a guide, for small bags cut from a 15.5–20cm (6–8in) square and for large bags from a 30–35.5cm (12–14in) square.

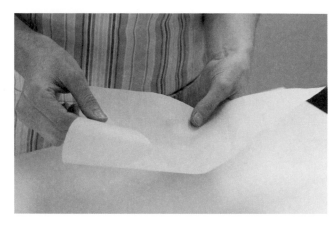

2 Keeping the centre point towards you with the longest side furthest away, curl the right-hand corner inwards and bring the point to meet the centre point. Adjust your hold so that you have the two points together between your right thumb and index finger.

3 With your left hand, curl the left point inwards, bringing it across the front and around to the back of the other two points in the centre of the cone. Adjust your grip again so that you are now holding the three points together with both thumbs and index fingers.

4 Tighten the cone-shaped bag by gently rubbing your thumb and index fingers forwards and backwards until you have a sharp tip at the end of the bag.

5 Carefully fold the back of the bag (where all the points meet) inwards, making sure that you press hard along the fold. Repeat this to ensure that it is really secure.

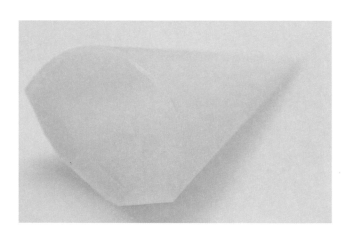

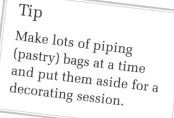

Tip

Make lots of piping (pastry) bags at a time and put them aside for a decorating session.

Piping with royal icing

For basic piping work, use soft-peak royal icing (see page 29). The size of the nozzle (tip) you use will depend on the job at hand and how competent you are. For most of the projects in this book I use a No. 1.5 plain nozzle (tip).

Fill the piping (pastry) bag until it is no more than one-third full. Fold the top over, away from the join, until you have a tight and well-sealed bag. The correct way to hold the piping (pastry) bag is important. Use your index finger to guide the bag. You can also use your other hand to guide you if it's easier.

To pipe dots, squeeze the icing out gently until you have the dot that's the size you want. Stop squeezing, then lift the bag. If there is a peak in the icing, use a damp brush to flatten it down.

To pipe teardrops, for small blossoms or leaves (see pages 108–109), once you have squeezed out the dot, pull the nozzle (tip) through the dot, then release the pressure and lift the bag.

To pipes lines, touch the nozzle (tip) down, then lift the bag up in a smooth movement, squeezing gently. Decrease the pressure and touch it back down to the point where you want the line to finish. Try not to drag the icing along, or it will become uneven. Use a template or a cookie outline as a guide where possible.

Working with flower paste

Flower paste is used for creating more delicate decorations for cakes and cookies, such as flowers, frills, bows and streamers, as it can be rolled out really thinly. Before using, knead the paste well by continuously pulling the it apart with your fingers.

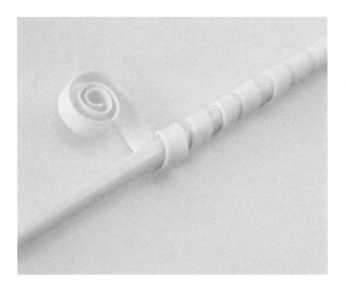

Modelling paste and CMC

Modelling paste is basically a stiffer version of sugar paste, which enables you to mould larger, less delicate shapes and objects. It isn't as strong and won't dry out as quickly as flower paste. You can buy ready-made modelling paste, but it is really simple and cheaper to make your own using CMC (sodium carboxymethyl cellulose). This comes in the form of a powder, which you knead into the sugar paste; use about 1 teaspoon per 300g (10½oz) icing.

Tip
Always add your colouring gradually and keep some extra white icing to hand in case you make a mistake.

Colouring icings

There are two types of colouring used to colour icing: paste and liquid. I prefer to use paste colours, especially when colouring sugar paste, flower paste and marzipan, to prevent the icing from becoming too wet and sticky. Small amounts can be added with a cocktail stick (toothpick) and larger amounts with a knife, then kneaded into the icing. Liquid colours work well with royal icing and liquid fondant, but be careful not to add too much too soon.

Be aware that the colour of your icing can often change as it dries. Some colours tend to fade, while others darken.

Creating streamers by winding strips of flower paste around thin plastic dowel (see pages 62–67).

Cutting holly leaves from green flower paste (see pages 110–116).

Making pink flowers from flower paste using two different sizes of five-petal blossom cutter (see pages 86–91).

Tip

It's always advisable to colour more icing than you need to allow for any mishaps, and quantities given in the recipes are generous. Any leftovers can be stored in an airtight bag in a sealed container for future use.

Basic cake recipes

It's important that your cake tastes as good as it looks. Always try to use the finest ingredients you can find, as this will make a big difference to the flavour. In order to achieve a professional, crust-free result, bake your cake in a tin 2.5cm (1in) bigger than the actual size you would like your finished cake to be. The sizes and quantities specified in the charts on the following pages will make cakes about 9cm (3½in) deep. For shallower cakes, miniature cakes and fondant fancies, use smaller quantities (see pages 20–21 and 24–25). For many of the projects in the book you can use any of the following cake recipes.

Equipment for cake making

- ✧ Greaseproof (wax) paper or baking parchment and tins
- ✧ Kitchen scales
- ✧ Measuring spoons and jug
- ✧ Large electric mixer
- ✧ 2–3 mixing bowls in different sizes
- ✧ Sieve (strainer)
- ✧ Spatula
- ✧ Palette knife
- ✧ Metal skewer
- ✧ Saucepan
- ✧ Large metal spoon
- ✧ Clingfilm (plastic wrap)

Classic sponge cake

For a really light sponge cake, it is better to separate the mixture between two tins. If you want three layers for your cake, split the mixture one-third/two-thirds. For smaller cakes, you can also cut three layers of sponge from a larger square cake. For example a 15.5cm (6in) round can be cut from a 30cm (12in) square cake (see opposite).

1 Preheat your oven to 160°C/325°F/Gas Mark 3 and line your tins (see page 12).

2 In a large electric mixer, beat the butter and sugar together until light and fluffy. Meanwhile, crack your eggs into a separate bowl. Add the eggs gradually, beating well between each addition. Then add the flavouring.

> ### Tip
> Make sure that the butter and eggs you are using are at room temperature before you start.

3 Sift the flour, add to the mixture and mix very carefully until just combined.

4 Remove the mixing bowl from the mixer and fold the mixture through gently with a spatula to finish. Tip the mixture into your prepared tin or tins and spread with a palette knife or the back of a spoon.

5 Bake in the oven until a skewer inserted into the centre of your cakes comes out clean. The baking time will vary depending on your oven. Check small cakes after 20 minutes and larger cakes after 40 minutes.

6 Allow to cool, then wrap the cake well in clingfilm (plastic wrap) and refrigerate until ready to use.

If cutting three layers from a larger square cake: for a 15.5cm (6in) round cake, bake an 8-egg/400g (14oz) butter etc. mix in a 30cm (12in) square tin; for a 13cm (5in) round or square cake, bake a 7 egg/350g (12oz) mix in a 20cm (11in) square tin; for a 10cm (4in) round or square cake, bake a 6-egg/300g (10½oz) mix in a 25.5cm (10in) square tin. For sculpted and carved cakes, add 10 per cent extra flour. See page 37 for additional flavourings.

Cake size	13cm (5in) round 10cm (4in) square 10–12 cupcakes	15.5cm (6in) round 13cm (5in) square	18cm (7in) round 15.5cm (6in) square	20cm (8in) round 18cm (7in) square	23cm (9in) round 20cm (8in) square	25.5cm (10in) round 23cm (9in) square	28cm (11in) round 25.5cm (10in) square
Unsalted butter	150g (5½oz)	200g (7oz)	250g (9oz)	325g (11½oz)	450g (1lb)	525g (1lb 3oz)	625g (1lb 6oz)
Caster (superfine) sugar	150g (5½oz)	200g (7oz)	250g (9oz)	325g (11½oz)	450g (1lb)	525g (1lb 3oz)	625g (1lb 6oz)
Medium eggs	3	4	5	6	9	10	12
Self-raising (-rising) flour	150g (5½oz)	200g (7oz)	250g (9oz)	325g (11½oz)	450g (1lb)	525g (1lb 3oz)	625g (1lb 6oz)
Vanilla extract (teaspoon)	½	1	1	1½	2	2	2½

Classic chocolate cake

This chocolate cake recipe is really quick and easy to make and has a lovely light texture. You should split the cake mixture between two tins, either dividing it equally or into one-third and two-thirds for three-layered cakes. Use a chocolate ganache filling rather than buttercream for a richer, more indulgent flavour (see page 43).

1 Preheat your oven to 160°C/325°F/Gas Mark 3 and line your tins (see page 12).

2 Sift the flour, cocoa powder (unsweetened cocoa) and baking powder together.

3 In a large electric mixer, beat the butter and sugar together until light and fluffy. Meanwhile, crack your eggs into a separate bowl.

4 Add the eggs to the mixture gradually, beating well between each addition.

5 Add half the dry ingredients and mix until just combined before adding half the milk. Repeat with the remaining ingredients. Mix until the mixture starts to come together.

6 Finish mixing the ingredients together by hand with a spatula and spoon into your prepared tins.

7 Bake in the oven until a skewer inserted into the centre of your cakes comes out clean. The baking time will vary depending on your oven. Check smaller cakes after 20 minutes and larger cakes after 40 minutes.

8 Leave to cool, then wrap the cakes well in clingfilm (plastic wrap) and refrigerate until ready to use.

Cake size	13cm (5in) round 10cm (4in) square 10–12 cupcakes	15.5cm (6in) round 13cm (5in) square	18cm (7in) round 15.5cm (6in) square	20cm (8in) round 18cm (7in) square	23cm (9in) round 20cm (8in) square	25.5cm (10in) round 23cm (9in) square	28cm (11in) round 25.5cm (10in) square
Plain (all-purpose) flour	170g (6oz)	225g (8oz)	280g (10oz)	365g (12½oz)	500g (1lb 2oz)	585g (1lb 4½oz)	700g (1lb 9oz)
Cocoa powder (unsweetened cocoa)	30g (1oz)	40g (1½oz)	50g (1¾ oz)	65g (2¼oz)	90g (3¼oz)	100g (3½oz)	125g (4½oz)
Baking powder (teaspoons)	1½	2	2½	3¼	4½	5¼	6¼
Unsalted butter	150g (5½ oz)	200g (7oz)	250g (9oz)	325g (11½oz)	450g (1lb)	525g (1lb 3oz)	625g (1lb 6oz)
Caster (superfine) sugar	130g (4½oz)	175g (6oz)	220g (8oz)	285g (10oz)	400g (14oz)	460g (1lb 1oz)	550g (1lb 4oz)
Large eggs	2½	3	4	5	7	8½	10
Full-fat (whole) milk	100ml (3½fl oz)	135ml (4½fl oz)	170ml (5¾fl oz)	220ml (8fl oz)	300ml (10fl oz)	350ml (12fl oz)	425ml (15fl oz)

Additional flavourings

For the classic chocolate cake:

Orange Use the finely grated zest of 1 orange per 2 eggs.

Coffee liqueur Add 1 shot of cooled espresso coffee per 2–3 eggs and add coffee liqueur to taste to the sugar syrup (see page 44).

Chocolate hazelnut Replace 10 per cent of the flour with the same quantity of ground hazelnuts and layer with chocolate hazelnut spread and ganache (see page 43).

For the classic sponge cake on pages 34–35:

Lemon Add the finely grated zest of 1 lemon per 100g (3½oz) sugar.

Orange Add the finely grated zest of 2 oranges per 250g (9oz) sugar.

Chocolate Replace 10g (¼oz) flour with 10g (¼oz) cocoa powder (unsweetened cocoa) per 100g (3½oz) flour.

Banana Replace the caster (superfine) with brown sugar. Add 1 overripe, mashed banana and ½ teaspoon mixed spice (apple pie spice) per 100g (3½oz) flour.

White chocolate cake

This white chocolate cake makes a lovely alternative to the classic chocolate cake, filled with luxurious white ganache (see page 43). If you find the recipe too sweet, add contrastingly tangy flavours such as lemon, lime or passion fruit (see opposite).

1 Preheat the oven to 150°C/300°F/Gas Mark 2 and line your tins (see page 12).

2 Break the chocolate into pieces, if using a bar, and put in a saucepan with the milk. Bring the milk slowly to the boil, stirring in the chocolate until it has all melted. Leave to cool.

3 In a large electric mixer, beat the butter and sugar together until the mixture is pale and fluffy. Meanwhile, crack your eggs into a separate bowl.

4 Add the eggs to the mixture, one at a time, beating well between each addition.

5 Sift the flour and baking powder together, add to the cake mixture and mix until just combined.

6 Pour in the chocolate mixture in two or three stages, depending on the size of the cake.

> ## Tip
> I prefer to use a spatula to fold the chocolate milk into the cake mixture to prevent it from slopping outside the bowl.

7 Pour the mixture into your prepared tins and bake in the oven for 20–50 minutes, depending on size. Check that the cake is cooked by inserting a skewer into the centre, which should come out clean.

8 Leave to cool, then wrap the cakes well in clingfilm (plastic wrap) and refrigerate until ready to use.

Cake size	13cm (5in) round 10cm (4in) square 10–12 cupcakes	15.5cm (6in) round 13cm (5in) square	18cm (7in) round 15.5cm (6in) square	20cm (8in) round 18cm (7in) square	23cm (9in) round 20cm (8in) square	25.5cm (10in) round 23cm (9in) square	28cm (11in) round 25.5cm (10in) square
White chocolate	170g (6oz)	225g (8oz)	285g (10oz)	365g (12¾oz)	505g (1lb 2oz)	590g (1lb 5oz)	705g (1lb 9oz)
Full-fat (whole) milk	185ml (6½fl oz)	250ml (9fl oz)	310ml (10fl oz)	400ml (14fl oz)	550ml (19fl oz)	650ml (22fl oz)	770ml (26fl oz)
Unsalted butter	115g (4oz)	155g (5½oz)	190g (6¾oz)	250g (9oz)	345g (12oz)	400g (14oz)	480g (1lb 1oz)
Caster (superfine) sugar	185g (6½oz)	250g (9oz)	310g (11oz)	400g (14oz)	550g (1lb 3½oz)	650g (1lb 7oz)	770g (1lb 11oz)
Medium eggs	2	3	4	5	7	8	10
Plain (all-purpose) flour	225g (8oz)	300g (10½oz)	370g (13oz)	485g (1lb 1oz)	665g (1lb 7½oz)	790g (1lb 12oz)	925g (2lb 1½oz)
Baking powder (teaspoons)	1	1½	2	2½	3½	4	5

Additional flavourings

For the white chocolate cake:

Lemon or lime Add the finely grated zest of 1 lemon or lime for every 2 eggs and lemon or lime curd when layering your cake.

Passion fruit Add strained and reduced passion fruit pulp to the white ganache filling (see page 43).

Traditional fruit cake

I have made many fruit cake recipes over the years, and this is one of my favourite ones. You can substitute the dried fruits with other dried fruits or keep it simple by using only pre-mixed dried fruit. Choose different types of alcohol to flavour your cake according to your own taste – I like to use equal quantities of cherry brandy and plain brandy. Rum, sherry and whisky also work well.

You need to soak your dried fruit and mixed peel in the alcohol at least 24 hours in advance. Ideally, your cake needs to be baked at least one month before it is to be eaten to allow it time to mature. You can also 'feed' your cake with alcohol once a week to keep the cake really moist and to enhance its flavour.

Tip

If you are making a large fruit cake, once you have incorporated the eggs into the mixture, you may need to transfer it to a large mixing bowl to mix in the remaining ingredients.

1 Preheat your oven to 150°C/300°F/Gas Mark 2 and line your tin with two layers of greaseproof (wax) paper or baking parchment for small cakes, and three layers for larger cakes (see page 12).

Tip

Make sure that the lining extends beyond the rim because standard cake tins are usually only 7.5cm (3in) deep and the cake will probably rise a little above the rim.

2 In a large electric mixer, beat the butter and sugar together with the lemon and orange zest until fairly light and fluffy. Add the orange juice to the soaked fruit and mixed peel.

3 Gradually add your eggs, one at a time, beating well between each addition.

4 Sift the flour and spices together and add half the flour mixture together with half the soaked fruit mixture to the cake mixture. Mix until just combined and then add the remaining flour mixture and fruit mixture.

5 Gently fold in the almonds and treacle (molasses) with a large metal spoon until all the ingredients are combined and then spoon the mixture into your prepared baking tin.

6 Cover the top loosely with some more greaseproof (wax) paper or baking parchment and then bake in the oven for the time indicated or until a skewer inserted into the centre comes out clean.

7 Pour some more alcohol over the cake while it's hot and leave to cool in the tin.

8 Remove from the tin and wrap your cake in a layer of greaseproof (wax) paper and then foil to store.

Cake size	10cm (4in) round	13cm (5in) round 10cm (4in) square	15.5cm (6in) round 13cm (5in) square	18cm (7in) round 15.5cm (6in) square	20cm (8in) round 18cm (7in) square	23cm (9in) round 20cm (8in) square	25.5cm (10in) round 23cm (9in) square
Currants	100g (3½oz)	125g (4½oz)	175g (6oz)	225g (8oz)	300g (10½oz)	375g (13oz)	450g (1lb)
Raisins	125g (4½oz)	150g (5½oz)	200g (7oz)	275g (9½oz)	350g (12oz)	450g (1lb)	555g (1lb 4oz)
Sultanas (golden raisins)	125g (4½oz)	150g (5½oz)	200g (7oz)	275g (9½oz)	350g (12oz)	450g (1lb)	555g (1lb 4oz)
Glacé (candied) cherries	40g (1½oz)	50g (1¾oz)	70g (2½oz)	100g (3½oz)	125g (4½oz)	150g (5½oz)	180g (6oz)
Mixed peel	25g (1oz)	30g (1oz)	45g (1¾oz)	50g (1¾oz)	70g (2½oz)	85g (3oz)	110g (3¾oz)
Cherry brandy and brandy mix (tablespoons)	2	2½	3	3½	5	6	7
Slightly salted butter	100g (3½oz)	125g (4½oz)	175g (6oz)	225g (8oz)	350g (12oz)	375g (13oz)	450g (1lb)
Brown sugar	100g (3½oz)	125g (4½oz)	175g (6oz)	225g (8oz)	350g (12oz)	375g (13oz)	450g (1lb)
Grated zest of lemon (per fruit)	¼	½	¾	1	1½	1¾	2
Grated zest of small orange (per fruit)	¼	½	¾	1	1½	1¾	2
Juice of small orange (per fruit)	¼	¼	½	½	¾	¾	1
Medium eggs	2	2½	3	4½	6	7	8½
Plain (all purpose) flour	100g (3½oz)	125g (4½oz)	175g (6oz)	225g (8oz)	350g (12oz)	375g (13oz)	450g (1lb)
Mixed spice (apple pie spice) (teaspoon)	½	½	¾	¾	1	1¼	1½
Ground nutmeg (teaspoon)	¼	¼	½	½	½	¾	¾
Ground almonds	10g (¼oz)	15g (½oz)	20g (¾oz)	25g (1oz)	35g (1¼oz)	45g (1½oz)	55g (2oz)
Flaked (slivered) almonds	10g (¼oz)	15g (½oz)	20g (¾oz)	25g (1oz)	35g (1¼oz)	45g (1½oz)	55g (2oz)
Black treacle (molasses) (tablespoons)	½	¾	1	1½	1½	1¾	2
Baking time (hours)	2½	2¾	3	3½	4	4½	4¾

Fillings and coverings

Fillings are used to add flavour and moisture to a cake and should complement the sponge mixture. Buttercreams and flavoured ganache are the two most widely used fillings and both recipes here allow cakes to be stored at room temperature so that they can be safely displayed rather than having to keep them in the refrigerator until ready to be eaten. Ganache is used for chocolate-flavoured cakes.

Buttercream and ganache are also used to seal and coat the cake before icing. They make a firm and perfectly smooth surface for the icing to sit on, filling in any gaps and imperfections in the cake. See page 45 for filling and covering quantities.

Buttercream

Makes about 500g (1lb 2oz), enough for an 18–20cm (7–8in) round or square layered cake, or 20–24 cupcakes

Materials

♦ 170g (6oz) slightly salted butter, softened
♦ 340g (11¾oz) icing (confectioners') sugar
♦ 2 tablespoons water
♦ 1 teaspoon vanilla extract or alternative flavouring (see below)

Equipment

✧ Electric mixer
✧ Scales
✧ Spatula

1 Put the butter and icing (confectioners') sugar in the bowl of an electric mixer and mix together, starting on a low speed to prevent the mixture from going everywhere.

2 Add the water and vanilla extract or other flavouring and increase the speed, beating the buttercream really well until it becomes pale, light and fluffy.

3 Store the buttercream for up to two weeks in the refrigerator in an airtight container.

Flavour variations

Lemon Add the finely grated zest of 1 lemon
Orange Add the finely grated zest of 1 orange
Chocolate Stir in 90g (3¼oz) melted white, milk or dark (semisweet or bittersweet) chocolate
Passion fruit Stir in 1 teaspoon strained and reduced passion fruit pulp
Coffee Add 1 teaspoon coffee extract
Almond Add a few drops of almond extract or to taste

Jams and conserves (jellies and preserves) can also be mixed in or used on top of a layer of buttercream, for example vanilla buttercream and raspberry jam filling.

Ganache

This rich, smooth filling is made from chocolate and cream. It is important to use good-quality chocolate, with at least 53 per cent cocoa solids, in order to achieve the best result.

Makes about 500g (1lb 2oz), enough for an 18–20cm (7–8in) round or square layered cake, or 20–24 cupcakes.

1 Put the chocolate in a bowl.

2 Bring the cream to the boil in a saucepan, then pour over the chocolate.

3 Stir until the chocolate has all melted and is perfectly combined with the cream. Leave to cool and cover.

4 Store for up to a week in the refrigerator.

White chocolate ganache

Use white chocolate in place of the dark (semisweet or bittersweet) chocolate and half the amount of cream. If you are making a small batch, melt the white chocolate before mixing with the hot cream.

> ### Tip
> Make sure that your ganache or buttercream is at room temperature before you use it – you may even need to warm it slightly so that it spreads easily.

Materials

♦ 250g (9oz) dark (semisweet or bittersweet) chocolate, chopped, or callets
♦ 250g (9oz) double (heavy) cream

Equipment

✧ Saucepan
✧ Mixing bowl
✧ Spatula

Sugar syrup

This is brushed on to the sponge to add moisture and flavour. The amount of syrup used is a personal choice. If you feel that your cake is quite dry, use more syrup. However, be aware that if you add too much syrup, your cake can become overly sweet and sticky. I recommend the following quantities for a 20cm (8in) layered round cake (you will need slightly more for a 20cm/8in square cake), 25 fondant fancies or 20–24 cupcakes.

Materials

♦ 80g (3oz) caster (superfine) sugar
♦ 80ml (2¾fl oz) water
♦ Flavouring (optional – see below)

Equipment

♦ Saucepan
♦ Metal spoon

1 Put the sugar and water in a saucepan and bring to the boil, stirring once or twice.

2 Add any flavouring and leave to cool. Store in an airtight container in the refrigerator for up to one month.

Flavourings

Vanilla Add 1 teaspoon good-quality vanilla extract
Lemon Replace the water with freshly squeezed, finely strained lemon juice
Orange Replace the water with freshly squeezed, finely strained orange juice

> ### Tip
> Liqueurs such as Grand Marnier, amaretto and limoncello can also be added to enhance the syrup's flavour.

Cake portion guide

The following guide indicates about how many portions you get from the different sizes of cake. The number of portions are based on them being about 2.5cm (1in) square and 9cm (3½in) deep. You may choose to allow smaller portions for fruit cake, as it's a lot richer.

Size	10cm (4in)		13cm (5in)		15.5cm (6in)		18cm (7in)		20cm (8in)		23cm (9in)		25.5cm (10in)	
Shape	o	sq	o	sq	o	sq	o	sq	o	sq	o	sq	o	sq
Portions	5	10	10	15	20	25	30	40	40	50	50	65	65	85

Filling and covering quantities

The chart below will give you a guide to how much buttercream or ganache you need to layer and cover different-sized cakes and cupcakes (see pages 42–43).

Size	10cm (4in)	13cm (5in) 10–12 cupcakes	15.5cm (6in)	18cm (7in)	20cm (8in)	23cm (9in)	25.5cm (10in)
Buttercream or ganache	175g (6oz)	250g (9oz)	350g (12oz)	500g (1lb 2oz)	650g (1lb 7oz)	800g (1lb 12oz)	1.1kg (2lb 8oz)

Daisy chain days

Pure, fresh and bright, daisies are the essence of springtime. These cheery little yellow-centred white flowers evoke fond memories of my childhood when my sister and I would spend hours in the garden making daisy chains as gifts for our mum. So what could be more fitting for a Mother's Day celebration than a combination of pretty, smiling daisy faces and fluffy, sumptuous buttercream scattered over another nostalgic favourite – the cupcake.

Celebrate the theme

As well as for Mother's Day, the daisy theme is ideal for any springtime celebration, whether it's Easter or a special birthday, and has appeal for children and adults alike. In fact, the kids could make some real daisy chains to decorate the place settings.

You could echo the cake board trimming by using the same ribbon tied around white napkins and a yellow gingham tablecloth to match, perhaps teamed with complementary-coloured blue and white china.

Provide further decoration for the setting with terracotta pots of larger daisy-type flowers like marguerites or gerberas in florist's foam, tied with gingham ribbon or raffia, or use mini watering cans for a fun look.

Springtime sensation

Lemon sponge cake is my flavour of choice here, as it perfectly reflects the theme – see page 37 for how to vary the classic sponge recipe with grated lemon zest – but vanilla also works really well. The homemade cake stand edged with yellow gingham ribbon has just the right clean, country look.

Materials

♦ Caster (superfine) sugar, 125g (4½oz) ♦ Yellow edible dust ♦ White royal icing, 50g (1¾oz) (see page 29) ♦ Yellow food colouring ♦ White flower paste, 150g (5½oz) ♦ One 15.5cm (6in) round classic sponge cake (see pages 34–35), filled with buttercream (see pages 12–13 and 42) ♦ 18 vanilla- or lemon-flavoured cupcakes, in plain paper cases (liners) (see page 22) ♦ Flavoured buttercream (see page 42)

Equipment

✧ Small paper piping (pastry) bag (see page 30)
✧ Piping nozzle (tip) No. 2 plain
✧ Greaseproof (wax) paper or baking parchment
✧ Large and small non-stick rolling pin
✧ Large non-stick board with non-slip mat
✧ Daisy cutter in two sizes
✧ Foam pad
✧ Ball tool
✧ Palette knife
✧ Three-tier yellow cake stand (see page 19)
✧ 2.5cm (1in) or 3.6cm (1½in) yellow satin ribbon
✧ 1.5cm (⅝in) yellow gingham ribbon
✧ 2.5cm (1in) white sheer ribbon
✧ Double-sided tape

1 Start by making all the daisies. Colour the caster (superfine) sugar with a small amount of yellow edible dust and colour the royal icing with yellow food colouring (see page 33).

2 To make the flower centres, fill the small paper piping (pastry) bag fitted with the No. 2 piping nozzle (tip) with the yellow-coloured royal icing and use to pipe balls on to greaseproof (wax) paper or baking parchment. While they are still wet, sprinkle over the yellow sugar. Leave to dry.

Tip

Break down the piping and sprinkling into smaller batches to avoid having to rush the sprinkling.

3 Roll out the white flower paste thinly with a large non-stick rolling pin on a large non-stick board set over a non-stick mat. Cut out the daisies in two sizes with your cutters – you will need about 100 for the top tier and six for each cupcake. Place the daisies on a foam pad and use the small end of your ball tool to press the centres of the flowers to make them slightly cupped so that the tips curl subtly upwards. Pipe tiny drops of royal icing on to the underside of the yellow flower centres and then carefully stick to each daisy.

4 For the large top cake, simply spread a thick layer of buttercream on to the cold cake with a large palette knife. Move the knife from side to side going around the side of the entire cake to create a neat and even pattern. Cover the top of the cake in the same way.

5 For the cupcakes, use a palette knife or knife to make a domed buttercream top on each (see page 22).

6 Decorate the cakes with your daisies. They will easily stick directly on to the buttercream without having to push them too far into the cake.

7 Complete your cake stand by wrapping some yellow satin ribbon around the centre columns (see page 19) and sticking yellow gingham ribbon around the edge of each board with double-sided tape (see page 17). You can secure the tiers with royal icing if you wish. Wrap a length of white sheer ribbon around the top cake and tie in a generous bow.

Daisy-sprinkle hearts

These delightfully dainty cookies are easy to make using a large heart cutter for shaping the cookie dough, then piping and flooding with yellow royal icing. They are trimmed with the same flowers as featured in the main cake, which you can vary from cookie to cookie, or decorate them all with the same design.

Pipe around the outlines of the baked cookies using the No. 1.5 piping nozzle (tip) and then flood with yellow-coloured royal icing using the No. 1 nozzle (tip) (see page 28). Make the daisies following the instructions for the main cake and stick in place as shown in the photo with a little royal icing.

You'll also need

Heart-shaped cookies, cut out with a large heart cutter (see pages 26–27)
♦ Piping nozzles (tips): No. 1.5 and No. 1 plain

Tip

Instead of dainty daisies, try making larger daisy-like flowers from deep pink or orange flower paste to look like gerberas, to decorate your cookies in bold style.

Baby's special sewing box

Patchwork conjures up a sense of home, comfort and family love – just the right sentiments for welcoming a new baby into the fold. The beautiful design of my daughter Maya's first cot quilt gave me the inspiration for this collection of cakes and cookies, perfect for a baby shower, christening or naming celebration. I have opted for a classic soft pastel colour scheme, with simple shapes and repeat patterns in keeping with the 'nursery' feel.

Celebrate the theme

Wrap pastel-coloured ribbon around your invitations and stick on a coordinating pastel-coloured button. The same treatment can be applied to place cards.

Extend the button theme by scattering them over the table or displaying them in pretty glass vases, dishes or jars. Team with pastel-coloured tableware and different pastel-coloured napkins for each place setting.

Tie matching-coloured bows on to the backs of chairs or around cake stands. Pastel-coloured patchwork cushions or fabric would finish off the look in style.

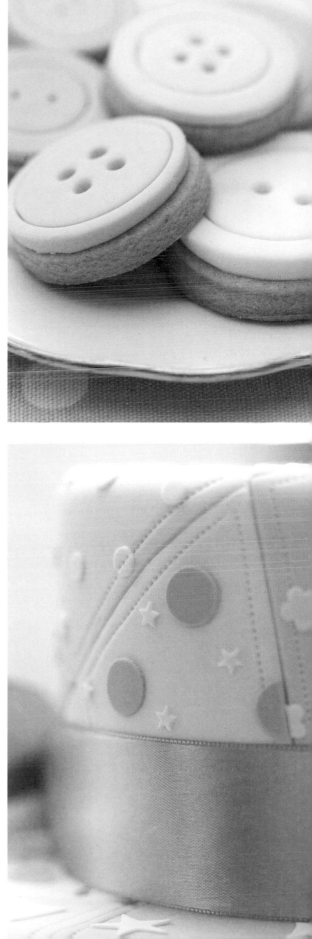

"Patchwork conjures up a sense of home, comfort and family love... just right for welcoming a new baby"

Pretty in patchwork

Pieces of coloured icing cut into irregular shapes are patched together with a stitching effect created using a sugarcrafting tool. Each piece of coloured icing is then decorated with a different motif – spots, stars, hearts, triangles and flowers. The combination of round and square tiers provides extra interest, with the large satin bow adding a softening touch.

Tip

Instead of using neutral tones, you could make the design in bright colours instead or introduce a bolder colour in the patterning.

Materials

One 13cm (5in) round and one 18cm (7in) square cake (see pages 34–41), covered with a thin layer of white sugar paste or marzipan (see pages 12–16) ♦ One 30cm (12in) round pale yellow iced cake board (see page 16) ♦ Sugar paste, 1kg (2lb 4oz) ♦ 1–2 teaspoons CMC ♦ Edible glue ♦ Flower paste, 250g (9oz) ♦ Food colourings: baby blue, cornflower blue, green, purple and yellow

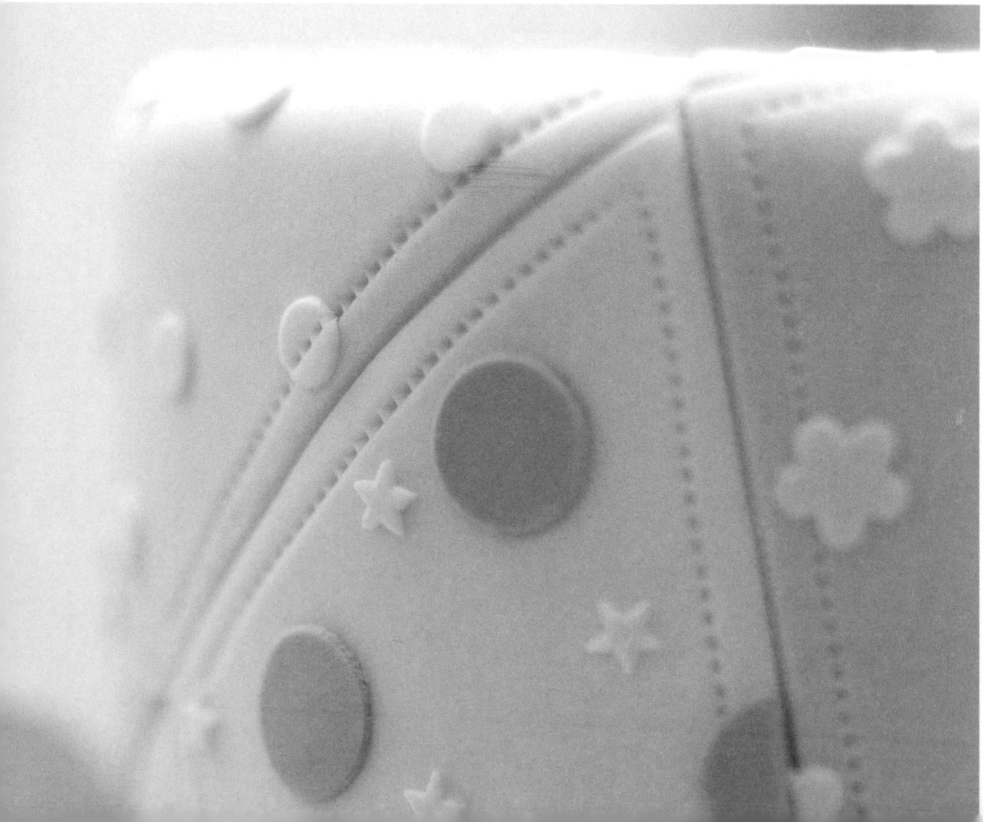

Equipment

- 3 hollow dowels
- Small plastic bags
- Small non-stick rolling pin
- Large non-stick board with non-slip mat
- Thin icing or marzipan spacers or strips of wood
- Large and small, sharp knife
- Stitching tool
- 3.5–4cm (1½in) green satin ribbon
- Fine paintbrush
- 2 small circle cutters in two different sizes
- Small plunger cutters: star and blossom
- Cutters: small triangle, star and heart
- Icing smoothers
- Piping nozzle (tip) No. 4 plain
- 1.5cm (5/8in) pale blue ribbon
- Double-sided tape

1 Dowel and assemble the two-tiered cake on your iced cake board (see pages 18–19). The round tier should be stacked directly on top and in the centre of the square tier.

2 Split the sugar paste into six equal pieces. Colour each piece so that you have pale blue and cornflower blue, pale green and a darker green (add more colouring), pale purple and pale yellow (see page 33). Knead a small amount of CMC (about $^1/_5$ teaspoon) into each coloured piece of sugar paste so that it becomes slightly stiffer (see page 32). Put each piece of icing into a plastic bag to prevent it from drying out.

3 Roll out some of the pale green sugar paste thinly with a small non-stick rolling pin on a large non-stick board set over a non-slip mat to about 2–3mm ($^1/_8$in) thick. Use thin spacers or strips of wood as a guide to the correct width. Using a large, sharp knife, cut an irregular shape about 5–6cm (2–2½in) square.

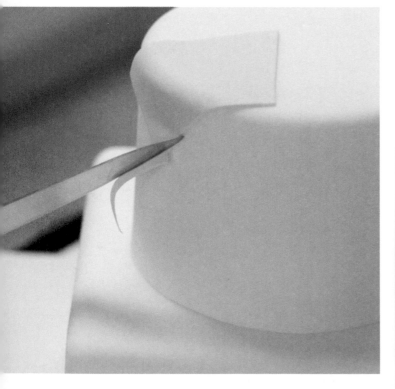

4 Stick the first patch on the top of the cake with a small amount of edible glue. Use a knife to trim any paste if the piece of icing has become misshapen.

5 Go around the inside of the shape a short distance from the edge with the stitching tool to mark a line of stitching.

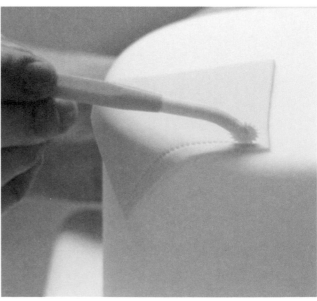

6 Roll out another colour of sugar paste and repeat the process. Working from the centre of the top tier, stick the other pieces of coloured icing on to the cake, cutting away any paste if necessary so that the patches fit well together. Work all the way around and continue to the bottom of the cake.

7 Carefully wrap the wide green satin ribbon around the base of the top tier and tie it in a big luxurious bow.

Tip

Make the stitching markings as you go, rather than all at the end, as the shapes will dry out quite quickly and you then won't be able to do them at all.

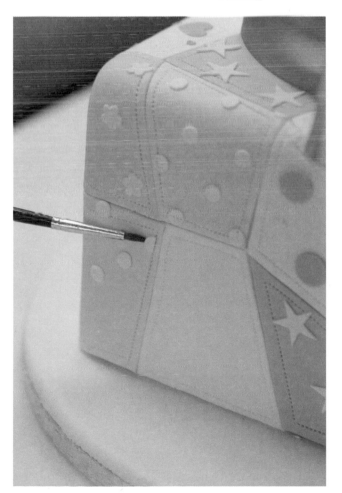

8 Split the flower paste into six equal pieces and colour each piece so that you have yellow, purple-blue, pale purple, pale green, pale blue and purple.

9 To decorate the palest green patches, cut out small circles from the yellow flower paste with a small circle cutter and stick them an equal distance apart on the patch with edible glue.

10 To decorate the pale blue patches, cut slightly larger circles with a circle cutter from the purple-blue flower paste and tiny stars using a plunger cutter from yellow flower paste. To decorate the purple patches, cut small blossoms using a plunger cutter from the pale purple flower paste. Position some of the shapes so that they extend beyond the edge of the patch. Trim with a sharp knife level with the patch edge before you stick in place with edible glue, to avoid denting the cake with the hard flower paste.

11 Go over any shapes where they cross the stitching with the stitching tool.

12 For the darker green patches, cut out triangles from yellow flower paste and small circles from the pale green flower paste using cutters. To decorate the darker blue patches, cut stars from pale blue flower paste using a star cutter. To decorate the yellow patches, cut hearts from the purple flower paste using a heart cutter and stick in place, spacing equally apart. Cut out very small circles from the purple flower paste using the end of a No. 4 plain piping nozzle (tip) and position between the hearts.

13 Finish by securing some 1.5cm (⅝in) ribbon around the base cake board with double-sided tape (see page 17).

Pastel pincushions

Each fondant fancy features one of the patterns used for the patchwork design on the main cake or is decorated with a little sugar button.

Dip the fondant fancies in pastel-coloured fondant (see pages 24–25) and decorate with flower paste shapes as in the patchwork cake. See opposite for instructions on making the buttons from sugarpaste.

You'll also need

Fondant fancies, in foil cases (liners) (see pages 24–25)

Cute-as-a-button cookies

These cookies can be made in variety of sizes and colours. Wrap in clear cookie bags and add a tag with the new arrival's name and date.

Use the cookie circle cutters to cut circles from rolled-out pastel-coloured sugar paste to cover each cookie (see page 28). Use slightly smaller cutters to make an indentation a short distance inside the edge of the circles. Brush a tiny amount of the masking spread or jam (jelly) on to the cookies and stick on the sugar paste circles. Make the buttonholes using the end of a No. 3 plain piping nozzle (tip) and the No. 4 nozzle (tip) used for the main cake.

You'll also need

Round cookies, cut out with circle cutters of different sizes (see pages 26–27)
- ◆ Boiled and cooled apricot masking spread or strained jam (jelly)
- ◆ Pastry brush
- ◆ Piping nozzle (tip) No. 3 plain

A birthday in technicolour!

It's often the traditional trappings of a good old-fashioned celebration that capture the party spirit and set the scene for fun and games. So instead of a birthday cake in the shape of a car or pirate ship, musical instrument or handbag, I've gone for those retro party-time favourites – streamers, stars and balloons – in unashamedly bright colours. These versatile designs will suit any age and gender.

Celebrate the theme

Decorate the party area with plenty of streamers and balloons in neon colours like pink, purple, orange and lime green.

Use large, rounded letters and bright psychedelic colours when making the party invitations to give a sixties or seventies feel.

For older birthday boys and girls, you could go the whole way by making it a sixties fancy dress party. Bright tie-dye and hippie-style table decorations, lighted joss sticks and vibrantly coloured fruit juices and 'mocktails' in fancy cocktail glasses would really get the party in the swing!

> "The traditional trappings of a good old-fashioned celebration capture the party spirit and set the scene for fun and games"

Celebratory streamers

The big and bold, almost neon-coloured streamers are the main feature
of this cake design. They are made simply by twisting long strips of icing
around a thin plastic dowel and are attached to the cake while semi-wet so
that they 'fall' into position. The chocolate icing makes a lovely contrast to
colourful streamers, but plain white icing would also work well.

Materials

One 13cm (5in) and one 20cm (8in) deep round cake (see pages
34–39), filled with buttercream or ganache and covered with chocolate-
flavoured sugar paste (see pages 12–15 and 42–43) ♦ One 28cm (11in)
round cake board, iced with chocolate-flavoured sugar paste (see page
16) ♦ A little stiff royal icing (see page 29 – optional) ♦ ¼ teaspoon
CMC ♦ Chocolate-flavoured sugar paste, 50g (1¾oz) ♦ Edible glue
♦ White flower paste, 350g (12oz) ♦ Food colourings: pink, yellow, blue,
green, purple and orange/tangerine

Equipment

✧ 3 hollow dowels
✧ 1.5cm (⁵⁄₈in) brown satin ribbon
✧ Double-sided tape
✧ Small non-stick board with
   non-slip mat
✧ Small non-stick rolling pin
✧ Small star plunger cutter
✧ Fine paintbrush
✧ Small and large, sharp knife
✧ Metal ruler
✧ Thin plastic dowel
✧ Small metal star cutter

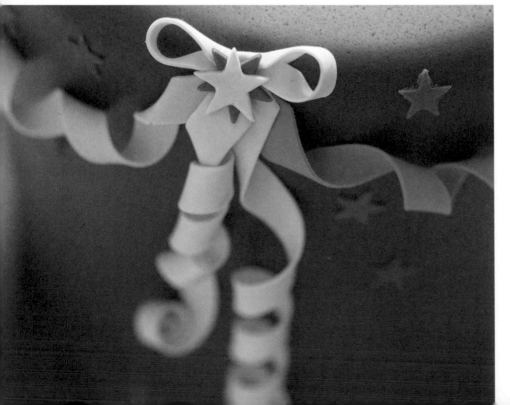

1 Start by dowelling the bottom tier of the cake and assemble the 2 tiers on the iced cake board (see pages 18–19).

2 Wrap some of the brown satin ribbon around the base of each tier and secure with double-sided tape or a little stiff royal icing.

3 Knead the CMC into the chocolate-flavoured sugar paste to make it stiffer (see page 32) and roll it out thinly with a small non-stick rolling pin on a small non-stick board set over a non-slip mat.

4 Cut small stars using the small plunger cutter. Stick them on to the cake in a random fashion around the tops of each tier with a small amount of edible glue.

5 Divide the white flower paste into six pieces and colour each one with a different food colouring, kneading the icing thoroughly (see page 33). Keep the colours as bright as possible.

6 To make the streamers, roll out a small amount of one of the flower paste colours into a strip about 20cm (8in) long. Cut an even narrow strip about 5mm (^{3}/$_{16}$in) thick from the paste and twist it around thin plastic dowel. Pinch the two ends together so that they come to a point and set aside to stiffen a little.

Tip

You can use the handle of a wooden spoon or a similar-sized cylindrical object instead to wind the flower paste strip around.

7 Mark six points around the bottom tier, an equal distance apart, and four points on the top tier – you can simply judge this by sight. Before the streamer is completely dry, stick it to the cake between two points using edible glue. Repeat with all the colours until you have streamers around both the top and bottom tiers.

8 Roll out more narrow strips in the different flower paste colours for the hanging streamers. Curl up one end and wrap around the dowel to stiffen before sticking on the cake. Roll more strips, 7.5cm (3in) long, for the bows and fold in the two ends, pinching in the centre to join.

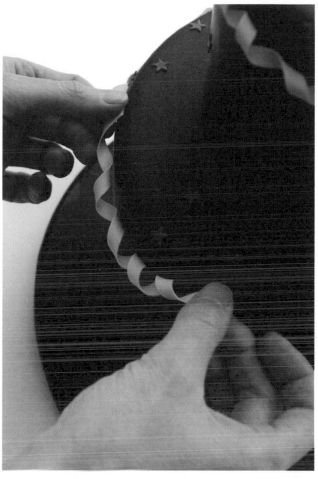

9 Cut out 10 brown and 10 coloured stars with the small metal cutter. Stick a brown star to each bow. Then stick a coloured star on top, in a matching colour to that of the hanging streamer, so that its points are positioned between the points of the brown star.

10 Finish off by securing more of the brown satin ribbon around the cake board with double-sided tape (see page 17).

Star-spangled cupcakes

These cupcakes make a perfect complement to the main cake, and are so easy to do that you can get the kids involved! Here I have used delicious chocolate buttercream to match the chocolate-coloured icing of the streamer cake, but you could also use vanilla or another flavour (see page 42).

Cut out stars from the different-coloured flower paste used for the streamers in the main project. Pipe an attractive buttercream swirl on to the cupcakes using a large plastic piping (pastry) bag fitted with a No. 1.5 star piping nozzle (tip) (see page 22). Decorate the cupcakes with the cut-out stars and sprinkles.

You'll also need

Chocolate cupcakes, baked in cupcake cases (liners) to match the theme (see page 22)
- Medium star cutter
- Chocolate buttercream (see page 42)
- Large plastic piping (pastry) bag
- Piping nozzle (tip) No. 1.5 star
- Mimosa sugar balls and other sprinkles

Balloon cookies

Add to the party mood with these cookies designed in the shape of balloons. I have used chocolate cookie dough to match the main chocolate-coloured cake, as it's such an effective contrast to the bright icing. Presenting the cookies on sticks to look like cookie lollipops adds to the fun.

Use the food colourings from the main project to colour the royal icing different colours for the balloons in advance. Start by outlining the cookies, then flood each in turn with runny icing and immediately drop spots of icing of a different colour on to the balloons (see pages 28–29). Leave the cookies to become completely dry before tying the ribbon around the bases.

You'll also need

Balloon-shaped chocolate-flavoured cookies, cut out with a cutter and baked on cookie sticks (see pages 26–27)

♦ Royal icing (see page 29)
♦ Small paper piping (pastry) bags (see page 30)
♦ Piping nozzles (tips): No. 1.5 and No. 1 plain
♦ Thin coloured ribbon

Summer seaside celebration

Nothing can be better guaranteed to evoke that sunny summer mood than the seaside theme – even if you have to retreat indoors from the rain! Here I've headed straight for the beach and majored on seashells, recalling many a carefree day spent beachcombing as a child. I have also incorporated pretty frangipani blooms to add an extra atmospheric touch, whose exotic fragrance I fondly remember from my time living on Australia's Sunshine Coast.

Celebrate the theme

Large conch shells placed on top of a clear, flat plate sprinkled with fine sand would form a lovely table centrepiece for the occasion. Scatter some smaller shells around the plate, along with dainty pieces of driftwood for unique table décor.

As alternative table decorations, half-fill small bowls with sand, add some pretty seashells to the top and insert a candle in the centre of each.

To add to the languid summertime ambiance, include hanging seashell wind chimes near open windows and doors. For atmospheric table lighting around the room, use seashell-shaped floating candles in bowls of aqua-tinted water.

“ Nothing evokes that sunny summer mood more than the seaside theme – even if you have to retreat indoors ”

Beachcomber's bounty

Tip

Both the seashells and the flowers can be made in advance and stored until you are ready to decorate the cake.

Two round cakes are carved into a bucket shape to incorporate shells, as a creative alternative to a traditional cake. I have used silicone moulds as a simple way to form the shells, which can be bought from sugarcraft or speciality chocolate suppliers. Using pearlized lustre dusts on the shells not only gives them an alluring, light-catching sheen, but also adds sophistication and finish to the cakes. The effect of sand is easily created by sprinkling on some brown sugar!

Materials

One 15.5cm (6in) and one 13cm (5in) round cake, each baked in two layers (see pages 34–39) ♦ Buttercream or ganache, 400g (14oz), plus extra filling, such as jam (jelly) or lemon curd, to go with the buttercream, if you like (see pages 42–43) ♦ White sugar paste, 750g (1lb 10oz) ♦ Food colourings: ice blue, caramel and brown ♦ Soft light brown sugar, 300–400g (10½–14oz) ♦ White flower paste, 400g (14oz) ♦ A little royal icing, for sticking (see page 29) ♦ White vegetable fat (shortening) ♦ Edible lustre dust: pearl white and mother-of-pearl ♦ Edible dusts: yellow, orange and ruby

Equipment

✧ Cake leveller
✧ 10cm (4in) round cake card
✧ Small and large, sharp knife
✧ Greaseproof (wax) paper or baking parchment
✧ Cake board or chopping board
✧ Large non-stick rolling pin
✧ Large non-stick board with non-slip mat
✧ Icing smoothers
✧ 20cm (8in) round thin cake board
✧ Palette knife
✧ Cake pedestal or serving plate
✧ Silicone shell moulds
✧ Dusting brushes
✧ Frangipani flower or medium tear-shaped cutter
✧ Foam pad
✧ Ball tool
✧ Cocktail stick (toothpick)
✧ Circle cutters, for the frangipani flowers to dry in

1 Start by carving the bucket-shaped cake. Level all four layers of sponge with the aid of a cake leveller until they are all about 4cm (1½in) high. Put the two smaller cakes directly on top of the two larger ones.

2 Place a 10cm (4in) round cake card on the top of the cakes and carefully mark around it with a knife. Gradually carve the sides of the bucket, slicing down from the top 10cm (4in) circle outwards right to the edge of the bottom cake.

3 When you have a good shape, layer and fill the cake with buttercream or ganache and any extra filling of your choice (see pages 12–13), placing it on a piece of greaseproof (wax) paper or baking parchment rather than a cake board. Cover the cake in a thin layer of buttercream or ganache (see page 14) and put it in the refrigerator for at least an hour or until it is firm.

4 Place the cold cake with the greaseproof (wax) paper or baking parchment on a spare cake board or chopping board. Colour the sugar paste with the ice blue colouring (see page 33). Roll out with a large non-stick rolling pin on a large non-stick board set over a non-slip mat to about 4–5mm (³/₁₆in) thick and use to cover the cake (see pages 14–15). Use the icing smoothers until the surface is flat and smooth, then trim away the excess sugar paste.

5 Roll out a long, thin sausage from the leftover sugar paste, then roll flat with the rolling pin to make a strip about 3cm (1¼in) wide. Wrap the strip round the base of the cake and cut away the excess.

6 Slice off the top (which is actually the bottom) of the cake and cover it with buttercream or ganache. Place the 20cm (8in) round thin cake board upside down on top of the cake and, using the board, carefully and swiftly turn the bucket up the right way. Remove the board and greaseproof (wax) paper or baking parchment from the top of the cake.

7 Using a palette knife, spread extra buttercream or ganache on the top of the bucket and a thick layer around the base, going out to the edges of the cake board. Carefully sprinkle over the brown sugar until the buttercream or ganache is covered. Set the cake on a pedestal or serving plate. Sprinkle the sugar around and over the edge of the board until completely hidden.

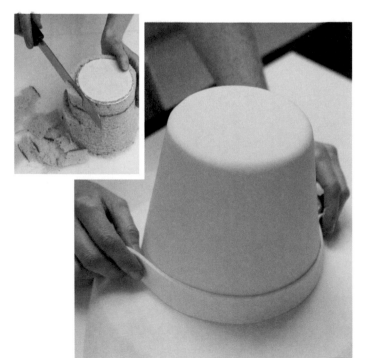

8 To make the handle, roll out some of the flower paste into a long, thin sausage about 25cm (10in) long. Using an icing smoother, gently flatten a little so that it is no longer completely round, to resemble a real bucket handle.

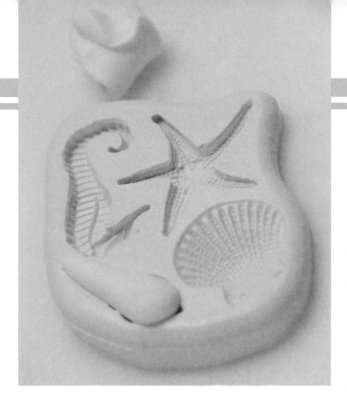

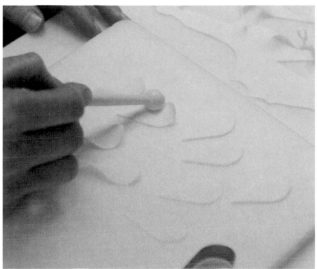

9 Set the handle aside until it becomes quite dry and holds it shape before sticking it to the cake with some royal icing. Roll two tiny balls of leftover ice blue sugar paste for the handle rivets.

Tip

You can pick up your handle and hang it around your bucket to measure that it is the correct length, then trim accordingly.

10 Make the shells one at a time, rubbing a tiny amount of white vegetable fat (shortening) inside the mould before you start. Knead caramel colouring into some of the remaining flower paste and roll a ball roughly the same size as the shell it will make. Press it into the mould and flatten the back. Remove the shell from the mould and put it aside to dry. Repeat, colouring the pieces of flower paste with varying strengths of caramel and brown colouring, until you have an assortment of shells. You will need 6–12 depending on the size of your moulds. Dust the shells with pearl white and mother-of-pearl edible lustre dusts.

11 To make the frangipani flowers, roll out the remaining flower paste very thinly and cut out five petals per flower using the frangipani or medium tear-shaped cutter. Place them on the foam pad and use the large end of a ball tool to soften the edges slightly. Use a cocktail stick (toothpick) to curl one side of each petal inwards.

12 Gather five petals together, overlapping each one along the flatter edge, keeping the flower closed. Glue and pinch together the bottom of the frangipani and then gently open out the petals. Put the flower in a circle cutter and leave to dry. Repeat with the other petals. Dust the centres of the flowers with yellow edible dust and add a little orange and ruby edible dust in the very centre to make a little darker.

13 Arrange the shells and frangipani flowers on top and around the bucket.

Life's a beach cupcakes

These convincingly sand-coated complementary cupcakes could be topped with any combination or varieties of shell. The delicately tapered, conical Florida auger and the familiar ridged scallop are two of my personal favourites. Others can be decorated with more gorgeous frangipani blooms.

Cover the buttercream-topped cupcakes with soft light brown sugar, as for the main cake, and decorate with more lustre-dusted flower paste seashells and frangipani flowers.

You'll also need

Cupcakes, baked in silver foil cases (liners) and topped with buttercream (see page 22)

Bathing belle and shell cookies

Here I've introduced a human, fun dimension in the form of bikini-shaped cookies, together with more shells and frangipanis.

Pipe around the outlines of the cookies and flood with white or ivory-coloured royal icing (see pages 33 and 28). Over-pipe details as shown in the photo with the No. 1.5 nozzle (tip). Add the little frangipani flowers by piping five small dots with the No. 1 nozzle (tip) and dragging the icing inwards to the centre of the flower (see page 31). Colour the flower centres by painting on some watered-down yellow food-colouring paste with a fine paintbrush.

You'll also need

Seashell, blossom and bikini-shaped cookies, cut out with cutters (see pages 26–27)

♦ Royal icing (see page 29)
♦ Food colourings: ivory and yellow
♦ Small and large paper piping (pastry) bags (see page 30)
♦ Piping nozzles (tips): No. 1.5 and No. 1 plain
♦ Fine paintbrush

Cherry blossom breeze

One of my favourite flowers, cherry blossom brings a breath of spring in all its pretty pink profusion. The delicate blooms ruffled by the breeze seem all the more precious because they are so short-lived. Inspired by Japanese fine art papers, these designs have a stylized, ornamental quality that gives them that special oriental flavour and sophistication.

Celebrate the theme

Cover the table in an oriental-style patterned fabric in colours to coordinate with the cakes and cookies, or opt for plain green or red runners placed across the table, overhanging the sides, and scatter with paper cherry blossoms.

Put an ornamental Japanese paper fan at each place setting, or try your hand at some simple origami folds for paper napkins.

Hang paper lanterns around the room to complement the lantern cookies. Depending on the occasion, you might like to serve tea Japanese style or sushi, using oriental tableware and chopsticks.

Cherry blossom
brings a breath of
spring in all its pretty
pink profusion

Oriental artistry

In keeping with the Japanese style, I have used square cakes with contrasting-coloured bands for their clean, angular lines. The appliqué techniques involved in making the blossom-decorated bands are one of my preferred ways to decorate a cake – easy yet highly effective.

Materials

♦ White flower paste, 300g (10½oz) ♦ Food colourings: pink, caramel, ruby and claret ♦ Royal icing, 50g (1¾oz) (see page 29) ♦ Gold edible dust ♦ Edible glue ♦ One three-layered deep 10cm (4in) and one deep 18cm (7in) square pale green iced cake (see pages 12–16, 34–39 and 42–43) ♦ One 25.5cm (10in) square white iced board (see page 16)

Equipment

✧ Small non-stick rolling pin
✧ Large non-stick board with non-stick mat
✧ Large five-petal rose cutters in two sizes
✧ Small and large, sharp knife
✧ Foam pad
✧ Ball tool
✧ Paper piping (pastry) bags (see page 30)
✧ Piping nozzle (tip) No. 1 plain
✧ Fine paintbrush
✧ Small circle cutter for the flower centres
✧ 4 hollow dowels
✧ Length of ribbon or measuring tape
✧ Metal ruler
✧ Plunger cutters: medium and small blossom
✧ 1.5cm (⅝in) green satin ribbon
✧ Double-sided tape

1 Start by making the large cherry blossom flowers to give them enough time to dry. Colour 75g (2¾oz) white flower paste deep pink (see page 33) and roll out fairly thinly with a small non-stick rolling pin on a large non-stick board set over a non-slip mat. Cut out two large flowers with the larger five-petal rose cutter. Cut out a V from each of the petals using a sharp knife.

2 Place each large flower in turn on the foam pad. Use the large end of your ball tool to press around the inside edge of the flowers so that the edges curl slightly upwards.

Tip

If the petals have become dry when it comes to sticking them together, use royal icing instead of edible glue to assemble them.

3 Repeat Steps 1 and 2 using the smaller five-petal rose cutter and white flower paste to make the inner petals. Leave to dry.

4 Pipe an outline around each with caramel-coloured royal icing using the No. 1 nozzle (tip) (see page 31), allow to dry, then paint with gold edible dust using a fine paintbrush. Stick the white petals on top of the pink petals with edible glue.

5 Colour 25g (1oz) white flower paste pale pink. Roll out and cut out two circles with the circle cutter. Stick one to the centre of each flower using royal icing. With the fine paintbrush, carefully paint some deep pink colouring in the centre of the flower to make the stamens. Finish by piping some dots with deep pink and ruby-coloured royal icing using your No. 1 piping nozzle (tip) (see page 31).

6 Dowel the 18cm (7in) cake (see pages 18–19) and stick this on to the centre of the iced cake board with royal icing. Leave the cake for a couple of minutes until it is secured in place before placing the 10cm (4in) top tier on to the centre of the larger cake.

7 Colour 150g (5½oz) white flower paste with the ruby and claret food colourings to make a deep raspberry colour. Roll a strip of paste long enough to fit around the base of the 10cm (4in) cake, using a length of ribbon or measuring tape to measure. Cut a strip about 3cm (1¼in) wide using a large, sharp knife and metal ruler. Repeat this process for the 18cm (7in) tier. Stick in position on the cakes with edible glue.

8 Roll out the remaining pale pink and deep pink flower paste left over from your larger cherry blossoms and cut out small blossoms with the medium plunger cutter. Colour half the remaining white flower paste medium pink, roll out and cut out some more blossoms. Colour the remaining white flower paste with the caramel colouring and use the small plunger cutter to cut out some more blossoms. Stick these on to the red bands around the tiers with edible glue. Decorate in between the flowers with piped dots of the caramel-coloured royal icing. Add gold dust to the caramel-coloured flowers and dots.

9 Stick the larger cherry blossoms on to the bottom and top cakes as shown in the photo with royal icing. Finish by attaching the green satin ribbon around the base board with double-sided tape (see page 17).

Tip

To make things easier for you, cut the strip into two sections and attach one at a time, joining the pieces at a corner or the back. Small blossoms can be positioned to conceal the join.

Springtime flower fancies

The varying shades of pink and red combined with green and gold featured in these fondant-iced and sugar paste-appliquéd miniature cakes is a traditional Japanese colour scheme.

Use the pink and ruby and claret food colourings from the main project, along with green, to colour the fondant icing (see page 33) and then use to cover the cakes (see pages 24–25). To decorate with the different designs, simply follow the instructions given for the main cake, using the medium plunger cutter to cut out blossoms from white, pale pink and deep pink flower paste. Decorate the flower centres and in between the flowers with piped dots of caramel-coloured royal icing, using a No. 0 piping nozzle (tip), dusted with gold.

You'll also need

Fondant fancies, in gold cases (liners) (see pages 24–25)
♦ Runny fondant icing (see page 23)
♦ Green food colouring
♦ Piping nozzle (tip) No. 0 plain

84

Exotic lantern cookies

These oriental-style lanterns create an alluring Eastern atmosphere hung from lengths of narrow ribbon in coordinating colours. I have used a chocolate cookie dough to stand out against the icing colours.

If you would like to hang your cookies, you need to carefully cut a small hole at the top as soon as soon as they come out of the oven when the dough is still soft. Pipe outlines and flood the cookies with green, pale pink and white royal icing (see pages 33 and 28). The blossoms are made with flower paste in the same way as for the cakes, using two sizes of five-petal rose cutter for the larger double blooms and the plunger cutters for the smaller single flowers. Add the piped details as shown using caramel-coloured and white royal icing and a No. 0 plain piping nozzle (tip).

You'll also need

Lantern-shaped chocolate-flavoured cookies, cut out with cutters (see pages 26–27)

♦ Green food colouring
♦ Tiny circle cutter (optional)
♦ Five-petal rose cutters in two sizes
♦ Small plunger cutters in two sizes
♦ Piping nozzle (tips): No. 1.5 and No. 0 plain
♦ Narrow ribbon, for hanging (optional)

A magical mad tea party

Lewis Carroll's weird and wonderful *Alice in Wonderland* story has the magical power to set the imagination free to explore a fantastical world, which is how I came to create this collection of whimsical cakes and cookies. Crooked and lopsided shapes, uneven bold and colourful patterns – this is your chance to run riot and have fun making these extraordinary confections, which are just as appealing to adults as children.

Celebrate the theme

Major on bright colours, with pinks, yellows and blues prominent. A vase of vibrant, surreal-looking red and white roses as the centrepiece would make the right impact.

Use doilies and tulle to decorate the place settings, choosing an eclectic mix of patterns such as stripes, checks, circles and other designs. Mismatched or oversized cups, plates and saucers can add to the sense of the absurd. Scatter the table with playing cards and chess pieces, along with labels or signs saying 'eat me' and 'drink me', or 'this way' or 'that way'.

Use a collection of odd chairs so that people are sitting at different heights around the tea table.

“ The weird and wonderful *Alice in Wonderland* story has the magical power to set the imagination free to explore a fantastical world ”

A wonky wonder

Like Alice's wonderland with its peculiar goings-on, this quirky cake design is full of beguiling irregularity, and was inspired by Disney's original movie dating back to 1951. The sloping tiers that taper in at the bottom reflect the style of the hat worn by the Mad Hatter himself.

Materials

♦ About 2 teaspoons CMC ♦ Coloured sugar paste (see page 33): pale purple, 300g (10½oz); pale pink, 850g (1lb 14oz); pale peach, 500g (1lb 2oz); very lightly tinted purple, 150g (5½oz); orange, 100g (3½oz); ruby, 75g (2¾oz); fuchsia pink, 150g (5½oz); pale yellow, 150g (5½oz); caramel, 20g (¾oz) ♦ 28cm (11in) round white iced cake board (see page 16) ♦ Edible glue ♦ White flower paste, 150g (5½oz)
♦ Food colourings: pink, purple, ruby and yellow ♦ White vegetable fat (shortening) ♦ One 13cm (5in) and one 20cm (8in) round cake, both 13cm (5in) deep and with three layers (see pages 34–39) ♦ One 7.5cm (3in) round, 6.5cm (2½in) deep piece of cake ♦ Buttercream or ganache, for filling and covering (see pages 42–43) ♦ Stiff royal icing, for sticking, plus a little soft-peak royal icing for piping (see page 29) ♦ 3–4 flower paste daisies, made as described in Steps 1–3 on page 50

Equipment

✧ Large non-stick rolling pin
✧ Large non-stick board with non-slip mat
✧ Small, sharp knife or craft knife
✧ 7.5cm (3in) round cake card or similar size template
✧ Saucer
✧ Large serrated knife
✧ Metal ruler
✧ One 15.5cm (6in) and one 10cm (4in) round thin cake board
✧ Board or tray
✧ Greaseproof paper (wax) paper or baking parchment
✧ Icing smoothers
✧ 3 hollow dowels
✧ Teardrop cutters
✧ Petunia flower cutter and hydrangea or blossom mould
✧ Crumpled foil
✧ Small paper piping (pastry) bag (see page 30)
✧ Piping nozzle (tip) No. 1 plain
✧ Medium and large five-petal blossom cutters
✧ Foam pad
✧ Ball tool
✧ 1.5cm (⁵/₈in) white satin ribbon
✧ Double-sided tape
✧ Pink trim (optional)

1 Knead ¼ teaspoon CMC into half the pale purple sugar paste (see page 32). Roll out thinly into a circle about 25.5cm (10in) in diameter. With a small, sharp knife or craft knife, cut a wiggly line around the circle. Carefully stick on to the iced cake board using a little edible glue. Set aside.

2 To make the saucer, colour 40g (1½oz) white flower paste pale pink and roll it out thinly. Cut out a 7.5cm (3in) circle using a cake card or template and press it into a saucer lightly greased with white fat. Set aside to dry.

3 Level the three layers of sponge for the two larger cakes with a large serrated knife and stick them together with buttercream or ganache (see pages 12–13). Refrigerate to firm up. Cut a slope from the top of the two chilled cakes (see page 14). The lowest point of the 13cm (5in) tier should be about 9cm (3½in) and the lowest point of the 20cm (8in) cake should be about 9.5cm (3¾in).

4 Turn the 20cm (8in) cake upside down and place the 15.5cm (6in) thin cake board on top in the centre. Little by little, cut all the way around the cake from the cake board at the top, slanting outwards to the bottom of the cake (see page 14). Turn the cake back up the right way and sit it on the 15.5cm (6in) cake board with some buttercream or ganache. Cover the cake with buttercream or ganache, place it on a board or tray and refrigerate to firm up.

5 Repeat this process for the 13cm (5in) tier, but positioning the 10cm (4in) cake board towards the edge of the lowest point.

6 The top teapot tier, using the 7.5cm (3in) cake, is prepared in the same way as the other two tiers, but not layered and making the sides slightly rounded.

7 Clean the work surface. Put the largest tier on a sheet of greaseproof (wax) paper or baking parchment next to where you are working. Roll out the pale pink sugar paste and use to cover the cake (see pages 14–16) – you will need to be extra careful that the icing doesn't tear around the top edge. Use your hands to cup the icing under the top edge, almost lifting the icing slightly upwards before smoothing it down and around to the base.

8 Repeat this process with the pale peach sugar paste for the 13cm (5in) tier and the lightly tinted purple sugar paste for the teacup.

9 Dowel the bottom tier of the cake (see pages 18–19), but in this case you will need to cut each dowel flush with the sloping top. Stick the bottom tier on top of the prepared iced cake board and leave to dry for a few minutes before stacking the middle tier on top.

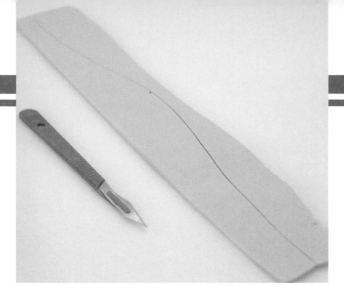

10 Knead ¼ teaspoon CMC into the orange sugar paste and roll out a long, thin strip about 2–3mm (⅛in) thick. Cut a straight edge down one side and a wavy line down the other. Stick around the middle tier, trimming and joining the ends with edible glue.

11 Knead ⅙ teaspoon CMC into the ruby sugar paste and roll out a long, thin sausage about 3mm (⅛in) thick. Use a small sharp knife to cut small, uneven pieces and roll them into balls. Stick them along the top edge of the orange collar with edible glue.

12 Knead ⅓ teaspoon CMC into the fuchsia pink sugar paste and roll out the coloured icing about 2–3mm (⅛in) thick and 14–16cm (5½–6¼in) long. Cut out wavy irregular strips and stick them one at a time around the cake, leaving gaps in between and trimming the strip neatly at each end.

13 Knead ⅛ teaspoon CMC into the pale yellow sugar paste and roll out to about 18cm (7in) in diameter, 2–3mm (⅛in) thick. Cut a wiggly circular shape in the same way as in Step 1. Drape it over the 13cm (5in) cake so that it hangs down like a tablecloth. Stick the dry saucer on top to one side with some royal icing.

14 For the tea cup, lightly tint about 50g white flower paste with purple colouring. Roll out half the amount into a long, thin sausage about 15cm (6in) long and 5mm (³⁄₁₆in) thick. Curl the ends round to make a handle and leave to dry before sticking to the teacup. Make the rim by rolling another sausage shape from the remaining purple flower paste and use icing smoothers to flatten it slightly on one side. Stick in place with edible glue. Cut out a circle of caramel-coloured sugar paste for the tea inside the teacup. Stick pale purple sugar paste teardrop shapes on to the side of the cup. Stick the teacup on to the saucer.

15 Cut out petunia flowers from thinly rolled-out ruby flower paste and shape them using a hydrangea or blossom mould. Allow to dry on some crumpled foil so that they keep their shape. Pipe their centres using yellow-coloured soft-peak royal icing and a No. 1 plain piping nozzle (tip) (see page 31).

16 Make the larger pink flowers by cutting out two different-sized blossoms from fuchsia pink-coloured flower paste using five-petal blossom cutters (see page 33). Frill the edges on a foam pad with the ball tool and stick the two sizes of blossom together with edible glue. Leave the flowers to dry with the petunias before rolling a ball of leftover yellow sugar paste for each centre.

17 Finish by sticking the flowers on the cake with some royal icing and trimming the cake board (see page 17).

Mad hatter minis

The playful mad mood of the tea party is extended here to these little hat cakes, some decorated to match the main cake and others crafted to look exactly like the Mad Hatter's hat.

Ice and decorate some of the miniature cakes using coloured sugar paste and flower paste as in the main project.

For the Mad Hatter's hat cakes, cover the miniature cakes with pale green-coloured sugar paste. Knead a small amount of CMC into some more pale green sugar paste (see page 32) and cut out 7.5cm (3in) circles for hat rims. Place on greaseproof (wax) paper or baking parchment and stick the hats to the rim centres. Use kitchen paper (paper towel) to shape either side of the rims and leave to dry. Wrap a strip of yellow flower paste around the base of each hat and cut out small circles from red flower paste with a No. 4 plain piping nozzle (tip) and a small circle cutter. Cut a label from white flower paste for each hat and paint on some squiggly lines to resemble writing with a fine paintbrush and slightly watered-down black food colouring or use a black edible pen.

You'll also need

Wonky-carved miniature cakes (see pages 20–21)

♦ Pale green-coloured sugar paste (see page 33)
♦ Kitchen paper (paper towel)
♦ Coloured flower paste: yellow and red
♦ Piping nozzle (tip) No. 4 plain
♦ Small circle cutter
♦ Black food colouring (optional)
♦ Fine paintbrush or black edible pen

Tea pot, tea cup and playing card cookies

The realistic-looking playing card cookies (see opposite) are drawn from another beloved bizarre scene in the *Alice in Wonderland* book where Alice encounters the Queen of Hearts. Team these with some more teacups and teapots.

For the playing cards, cover the cookies with white sugar paste cut to the same size (see page 28). Use the playing card cutters to cut suit shapes from red and black flower paste. Paint the numbers on with a fine paintbrush using food colouring very slightly thinned with water.

Cut out the decorations for the other cookies from white, purple and fuchsia pink flower paste using the teardrop cutters from the main project and small blossom and frill cutters. Pipe around the outlines with white, pink and purple-coloured royal icing, then flood with icing (see page 28). Add the extra piped details and stick on the flower paste decorations.

You'll also need

Rectangular-shaped cookies, about 6 x 9cm (2½ x 3½in), and teapot and teacup cookies, cut out with cutters (see pages 26–27)

♦ White sugar paste
♦ Playing card cutters
♦ Coloured flower paste (see page 33): red, black, purple and fuchsia pink
♦ Food colourings: red and black
♦ Fine paintbrush
♦ Cutters: small blossom and frill
♦ Piping nozzle (tip) No. 1.5 plain

Dressed all in white

Trends come and go, but a white wedding is enduringly elegant, and the bride's dress is of course the most precious, gorgeous element. Which is why brides often come to me with images of their dress as a source of inspiration for their cake. Here I have chosen classic lace detailing, presented on 'floating' tiers that allow it to hang down just as on a wedding dress, and in delicate butterflies that hover over dainty doily-like cakes.

Celebrate the theme

Cover the table with a pretty lace tablecloth or keep it plain and decorate with a lace runner. If you want to introduce a subtle element of colour, put a coloured tablecloth underneath to show through the lace.

Laser-cut stationery or place cards and menus with lace detailing would make the perfect accompaniment. And why not add laser-cut paper butterflies to the rims of glasses for a stunning finishing touch?

Crystal glassware and fresh flowers in cut-glass vases would complete the classic, cleanly radiant scene.

❝ A white wedding is
enduringly elegant,
and the bride's dress
is the most precious,
gorgeous element **❞**

A cascade of lace

Tip

If you want to introduce some colour, either wrap some coloured ribbon around the boards in the gaps, or colour the base icing for the cake – pale pink, for example.

The effect of lace can be recreated in icing in many ways using piping, brushwork or an appliqué technique, but here I have kept it really simple by using these fabulous lace moulds. Once pushed into the mould, removed and brushed with edible lustre, the flower paste really looks like a beautiful piece of lace. The cakes are assembled and dowelled in a similar fashion to stacked cakes, but cake boards are added between the tiers.

Materials

♦ Royal icing, 150g (5½oz) (see page 29) ♦ One 23cm (9in), one 18cm (7in) and one 13cm (5in) square white iced cake (see pages 34–43 and 12–16) ♦ One 30cm (12in) or 33cm (13in) square white iced cake board (see page 16) ♦ White flower paste, 400g (14oz) ♦ Pearl white edible lustre dust ♦ Edible glue ♦ A little clear alcohol, such as gin or vodka, or dipping solution

Equipment

✧ Two 10cm (4in), two 15.5cm (6in) and two 20cm (8in) square cake boards
✧ 8 hollow dowels
✧ Ruler
✧ 2.5cm (1in) ivory satin ribbon (optional)
✧ 1.5cm (5/8in) ivory satin ribbon
✧ Double-sided tape
✧ Icing smoothers
✧ Small non-stick rolling pin
✧ Large non-stick board with non-slip mat
✧ Dusting brush
✧ Scalloped border lace mould
✧ Small, sharp knife
✧ Selection of silicone lace moulds
✧ Small paper piping (pastry) bag (see page 30)
✧ Piping nozzle (tip) No. 1 plain
✧ Fine paintbrush

1 Stick the two 10cm (4in) cake boards together with stiff royal icing and put them aside to dry. Do the same with the two 15.5cm (6in) and the two 20cm (8in) cake boards as well.

2 Meanwhile, dowel the bottom 23cm (9in) and middle 18cm (7in) tier (see pages 18–19).

3 Stick the 20cm (8in) cake boards in the centre of your iced base cake board with stiff royal icing, checking their position by measuring with a ruler. Choose where the back of your cake will be and, starting at the back, wrap some ribbon around the two boards. You can either use 2.5cm (1in) ribbon or you can go around twice with 1.5cm (^{5}/8in) ribbon, slightly overlapping the ribbon. Secure the ribbon with double-sided tape.

4 Carefully place the largest cake tier on top of the 20cm (8in) boards. Again, use a ruler to check its position – you can move the cake a little using icing smoothers to push on the sides.

5 Repeat this procedure for the middle and top tiers, checking that the cakes and boards are in the centre as you go.

6 Start the lace work by making the bottom trim around each tier. Roll out some white flower paste thinly with a small non-stick rolling pin on a large non-stick board set over a non-slip mat until the length of the scalloped mould. Cut strips about 2.5cm (1in) wide.

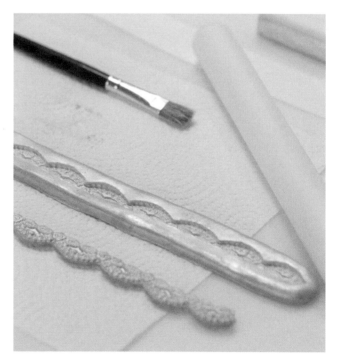

7 Brush some edible lustre dust on to both parts of the mould with a dusting brush and press a strip of flower paste top side down into the bottom part of the mould. Press the top piece of the mould into the bottom piece, with the flower paste in between. Carefully tear away the excess paste around the lace shape while pressing down firmly on the top of the mould.

9 To make the other pieces of lace, use silicone lace moulds and follow Steps 6–8, but cut the flower paste into pieces of a similar shape to the moulds you are using. Cut smaller pieces and individual blossoms from the lace icing once it has been removed from the mould.

10 Work from the bottom of each tier and complete each step around the whole cake on each tier. The lacework should continue over the top edge of each tier, but thin out nearer the top, with just a few lace motifs on top.

11 To finish the lacework, pipe some small white dots all over the cake using a small piping (pastry) bag filled with soft-peak royal icing and a No. 1 nozzle (tip) (see page 31). Once the dots are dry, mix the lustre with a few drops of clear alcohol or dipping solution to the consistency of paint and brush on to the dots with a fine paintbrush.

12 Finally, attach the 1.5cm (5/8in) ribbon around the base cake board with some double-sided tape (see page 17).

8 Remove the flower paste from the mould. You may need to use a small, sharp knife to help the icing release from the mould without tearing it. Brush the piece of lace icing with extra lustre dust if necessary. Stick the lace strip on to the cake with edible glue. Repeat the process with more strips of lace until you have a border around each tier. Stick the pieces of lace icing together neatly so that the joins aren't too noticeable.

Butterfly doily cakes

The pretty butterflies on these delicate miniature cakes are made using silicone lace moulds, as in the main cake. The moulds here are designed to make butterflies that are stuck directly on to the icing, but here I have cut out the wing shapes and then, after drying, stuck them together with royal icing piped to form the butterfly's body.

Cut the rolled-out flower paste and press it into the lustre-dusted butterfly lace mould as described in the main project. Trim the wings with a sharp knife or pair of small, sharp scissors until you have a nice shape. Set the wings aside to dry for 10 minutes.

You'll also need

Square miniature cakes, covered with white sugar paste (see pages 20–21)

♦ Butterfly lace mould
♦ Greaseproof (wax) paper or baking parchment
♦ A4 sheet of card folded concertina style

To assemble the butterflies, make a fold down two long strips of greaseproof (wax) paper or baking parchment and put each into a fold of the concertina-folded card. Using the No. 1 plain piping nozzle (tip), pipe a short line of royal icing down the centre of each and stick together two wings. Pipe the head and body of the butterfly and leave to dry completely before removing from the greaseproof (wax) paper or baking parchment. Attach the butterflies to the cakes with some stiff royal icing.

Wedding cake cookies

Cookies in the shape of a traditional three-tiered wedding cake and iced and decorated all in white to match the main cake are a lovely idea and are great to give to guests as favours. Put in clear bags and tie some lace or ribbon around the top. You could also attach a butterfly-shaped label if you want to continue the butterfly theme.

Use a piping (pastry) bag filled with soft-peak royal icing and the No. 1 plain piping nozzle (tip) to pipe a swag border along the bottom of each tier. Pipe tiny white dots at even intervals all over the cookies (see page 31).

You'll also need

Wedding cake-shaped white royal-iced cookies, cut out with a cutter (see pages 26–29)
♦ Clear cookie bags and lace or ribbon ties (optional)

A secret garden party

The idea of a summer celebration, whether for a wedding, anniversary or special birthday, on the theme of a secret garden instantly weaves its own magical, romantic atmosphere. It draws me back to the intricate and whimsical patterns of the past, as in this period-style birdcage design, with its intertwined flowers. Its decorative ironwork effect is then echoed in the complementary cupcakes and cookies. The dusky colours add to the vintage feel.

Celebrate the theme

Your secret garden party doesn't have to be an alfresco affair – with the right decorative elements, you can bring the outdoor theme into a conservatory or house to help with the practicalities.

An old lace or embroidered linen tablecloth would be perfect for the romantic, vintage feel, or choose a retro sprigged floral cotton fabric. Team with dainty floral-patterned china.

Pick up on the flowers in the designs and choose stems of blossom, garden roses or other traditional cottage garden flowers with foliage, instead of florist's flowers, and set them informally in old-fashioned vases or pretty wine glasses.

"a secret garden instantly weaves its own magical, romantic atmosphere"

Songbird sanctuary

The bars of the birdcage are easily recreated using strips cut from brown sugar paste and long, fine sausage shapes rolled from a mix of sugar and flower paste. The roses are also formed from sausage shapes cut into short lengths, and the white blossoms are cut-outs simply folded.

Materials

♦ Royal icing, 200g (7oz) (see page 29) ♦ Food colourings: dusky pink, baby blue, brown and green ♦ One 15.5cm (6in) round cake with three layers, each about 4cm (1½in) deep, and a 15.5cm (6in) half-sphere cake, baked in a purpose-designed baking tin (see pages 34–39)
♦ Buttercream, for filling and covering (see page 42) ♦ White flower paste, 150g (5½oz) ♦ White vegetable fat (shortening), for greasing
♦ Dusky pink edible dust ♦ White sugar paste, 1.25 kg (2lb 12oz)
♦ One 23cm (9in) round pale grey iced cake board (see page 16)
♦ ½–1 teaspoon CMC ♦ Edible glue ♦ Chocolate sugar paste, 100g (3½oz)

Equipment

✧ Small paper piping (pastry) bags (see page 30)
✧ Piping nozzles (tips): No. 1.5 and No. 1 plain
✧ 15.5cm (6in) round cake board
✧ Palette and small, sharp knife
✧ Cellophane sleeve
✧ Small and large non-stick rolling pin
✧ Large non-stick board with non-slip mat
✧ Blossom cutter
✧ Greaseproof (wax) paper or baking parchment
✧ Icing smoothers
✧ Small, sharp scissors
✧ 1.5cm (⅝in) pale blue satin ribbon
✧ Double-sided tape

1 To make the bird, follow the instructions for run-outs on page 29, using the template on page 126 and royal icing coloured dusky pink – 30g (1oz) for outlining using the No. 1.5 nozzle (tip) and 50g (1¾oz) for flooding using the No. 1 nozzle (tip). Leave to dry. Pipe over the outline again and add swirls for the wing and tail, using another 30g (1oz) icing.

2 To make the domed-shaped cake, use buttercream to stick the half-sphere cake on top of the round cake and place on the 15.5cm (6in) cake board. Cover the whole cake with a thin layer of buttercream using a palette knife as you would for a round cake (see page 14). Place in the refrigerator for 30–45 minutes to firm up.

3 To make the roses, roll a long, thin sausage of white flower paste and cut small pieces about 2–3cm (¾–1¼in) in length. Cut the cellophane sleeve so that it is joined down one long side only, open out and grease with white vegetable fat (shortening) to prevent sticking. Lay the sausages on the cellophane and close the sleeve up again. Press down on one edge to make indentations along each small sausage, leaving the other side fairly thick.

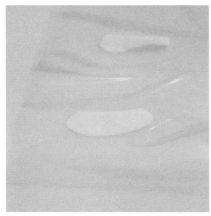

Tip

In addition to the bird decoration, you can also make the roses and white blossoms in advance.

4 Take each piece at a time and roll one end inwards to form your rose. Pinch at the bottom and pull away any excess paste. When you have made all the roses (you will need about 10–12 for the main cake), brush the top edge with dusky pink edible dust and set aside to dry.

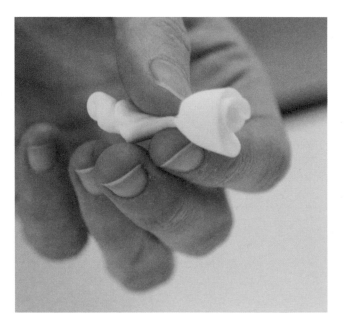

5 To make the little white blossoms, roll out some white flower paste thinly and cut out blossom shapes using a blossom cutter. Fold each blossom in half and half again. Pinch at the bottom and remove some of the stem. Make about 20 for the main cake. Leave to dry with the roses.

6 Colour all but 150g (5½oz) white sugar paste with a small amount of baby blue colouring (see page 33). Place your cold cake on some greaseproof (wax) paper or baking parchment. Roll the sugar paste out until the piece is big enough to cover the whole of the cake. Once the icing is on the cake, use your hands and then the icing smoothers to work the icing down to the bottom of the cake. You need to bring the paste inwards and slightly upwards as you go so that the weight of the paste doesn't cause it to tear. Trim away the excess paste and carefully lift the cake off the paper and on to the iced cake board, sticking it down with some royal icing.

7 To make the horizontal flat bars of the cage, colour the remaining 150g (5½oz) white sugar paste with brown colouring mixed with the CMC to strengthen it (see page 32). Roll out thinly and cut 5mm- (³/₁₆in-) wide strips. Stick around the cake with edible glue, joining the pieces together as neatly as possible.

8 To make the rounded bars of the cage, mix the chocolate sugar paste with 100g (3½oz) white flower paste coloured with brown colouring. Roll more long, thin sausage shapes using a icing smoother so that they are even. Cut pieces about 25cm (10in) in length. Stick one end of a piece in place at the base of the cake with edible glue and trim the other end where it meets the top centre point of the dome. Repeat all around the cake at about 3cm (1¼in) intervals.

9 To make the scrolled pieces, roll shorter sausage shapes from the remaining paste and curl into shape. Leave the pieces for about five minutes until hardened a bit but still pliable before attaching them to the cake with edible glue. Roll two balls from the leftover paste, one slightly smaller than the other, and attach to the top of the cage.

10 Colour the remaining royal icing with green colouring. Put into a small paper piping (pastry) bag. Carefully snip a small hole in the tip and pipe the climbing rose stems up the side and dome of the cake. Cut a V in the tip of the bag and pipe the leaves, attaching the roses and white blossoms as you go. Create a little ledge with some flowers for the bird to sit on. Attach the bird to the cake with some royal icing. Finish by attaching your ribbon around the cake board with double-sided tape.

Flower garden cupcakes

These elegant little fondant-iced and piped cupcakes adorned with dainty summer blooms complement the main cake perfectly, but are also gorgeous enough to take centre stage.

Divide the fondant in half and colour one portion baby blue and the other dusky pink (see page 33). Dip the cupcakes in the different-coloured fondant and leave to dry (see page 23). Colour some soft-peak royal icing with brown colouring and pipe lines with a No. 1 piping nozzle (tip) from the centre of the cake to the outer edge at even intervals all round each cake (see page 31). Attach three white blossoms to the centre of each pink cake and three roses to the centre of each blue cake, made in the same way as for the main cake. Pipe the leaves as for the main cake. Decorate the brown piped lines with blossoms created by piping small dots and teardrops of white royal icing (see page 31) and piped green-coloured royal icing leaves as for the main cake.

You'll also need

Cupcakes, in silver cases (liners) (see page 22)
♦ Runny fondant (see page 23)

Vintage gate and cage cookies

The scrolled ironwork of the birdcage cake is again featured here in these charming cookies, this time piped on to a flooded-icing surface and embellished with dainty piped flowers.

Colour some royal icing with baby blue food colouring and some with pale grey colouring (see page 33). Pipe an outline around the domed shaped of each cookie, then flood the birdcages with the baby blue and the gates with the pale grey icing (see page 28). Once they are dry, use brown-coloured royal icing and your No. 1 plain piping nozzle (tip) to pipe lines and scrolls as shown in the photo. Use some dusky pink-coloured royal icing to pipe tight swirls for the roses, white icing to pipe small dots and teardrops for the blossoms and green-coloured icing to pipe teardrops for the leaves (see page 31).

You'll also need

Birdcage and garden gate-shaped cookies, cut out using the template on page 126 (see pages 26–27)

♦ Pale grey food colouring

A giftwrapped Christmas

The festive season is all about family and home, and it always takes me back to making Christmas cakes with my mum and all the warm feelings associated with things homemade and traditional. I also remember the excitement and satisfaction of wrapping gifts in wonderfully colourful paper. So here I've drawn my inspiration from all those intoxicating Christmas wrappings, ribbons and trimmings, while keeping to classic red and white as the main colours.

Celebrate the theme

To echo the red and white colour scheme, cover the table with a brilliant, crisp white tablecloth and decorate with red or gold-coloured table runners, napkins and crackers.

A candle centrepiece and natural candlelight would be in perfect keeping with the traditional, heart-warming feel of the cake and cookie designs, decorated with sprigs of holly and ribbon loops, secured with thin wire, to echo the details of the designs. Rich red or green-coloured glasses and cake plates would complete the look.

Add to the festive atmosphere by hanging coloured baubles around the room, or opt for a nostalgic touch with retro honeycomb paper decorations.

"I remember the excitement and satisfaction of wrapping gifts in wonderfully colourful paper"

Gorgeous gifts

This fun design makes a show-stopping alternative to the traditional Christmas cake, with a cute little gift box stacked on top of a wrapped present. Both are dotted with simple cut-out flower paste shapes to resemble printed giftwrap, but for an extra flourish I have created an easy-to-make yet showy looped bow decoration for the top of the gift box.

Materials

♦ One 18cm (7in) square fruit cake (see pages 40–41), covered with marzipan and red sugar paste (see pages 14–16) ♦ One 10cm (4in) square fruit cake (see pages 40–41), covered with marzipan and white sugar paste (see pages 14–16) ♦ One 30cm (12in) round white iced cake board (see page 16) ♦ ½ quantity royal icing (see page 29) ♦ A little red and white sugar paste, for filling in cracks if needed ♦ White flower paste, 200g (7oz) ♦ Edible glue ♦ Red flower paste, 200g (7oz) ♦ Food colourings: green and brown

Equipment

✧ 4 hollow dowels
✧ Icing smoothers
✧ Red ribbon for bottom tier and white ribbon for top tier (optional)
✧ Small non-stick rolling pin
✧ Large non-stick board with non-slip mat
✧ Large and small, sharp knife
✧ Small circle cutter
✧ Holly cutter
✧ Paper piping (pastry) bags (see page 30)
✧ Piping nozzles (tips): No. 4 and No. 1 plain
✧ Greaseproof (wax) paper or baking parchment
✧ Fine paintbrush
✧ 1.5cm (⅝in) white satin ribbon
✧ Double-sided tape

1 Dowel the larger cake and stick it on the iced cake board with some stiff royal icing (see pages 18–19). Stick on the top tier and, using two icing smoothers, twist it so that it is at a different angle from the base cake, to make it look like it has been stacked naturally.

2 If the bases of your cakes are a little untidy, wrap some red ribbon around the bottom tier and white ribbon around the top tier to neaten. Alternatively, fill in any cracks with red or white sugar paste watered down to a wet putty-like consistency.

3 To make the 'ribbon' trimming for the bottom tier, roll out some white flower paste thinly with a small non-stick rolling pin on a large non-stick board set over a non-slip mat. Cut out four shaped strips about 15cm (6in) long and 2.5cm (1in) wide using a large, sharp knife.

4 Place the strip at the bottom of the cake and drape it over the top to measure the correct length before you trim and stick it in position with edible glue – it should come right up to the bottom of the top tier. Repeat this on all four sides of the cake.

5 To make the 'ribbon' trimming for the top tier, roll out four strips of red flower paste about 13cm (5in) long and 2cm (¾in) wide. Stick them on the cake as in Step 4.

6 To decorate the bottom tier, roll out some white flower paste and cut out small circles, using a circle cutter. Stick them to the cake around the trimming so that they are spaced evenly apart in a polka-dot fashion.

7 To decorate the top tier, colour 100g (1oz) white flower paste with green colouring (see page 33) and roll it out thinly. Cut holly shapes using the holly cutter and stick them to the cake with some edible glue. You will need to trim some of the shapes using a small, sharp knife where they meet the 'ribbon' trimming so that it looks as though the 'pattern' continues underneath.

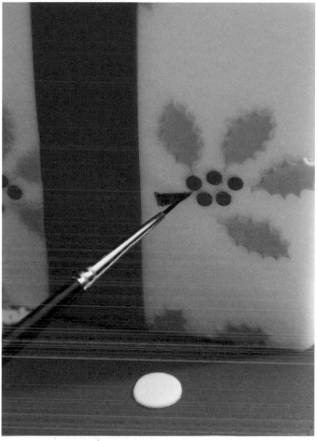

12 Finish by attaching the white satin ribbon around the cake board with double-sided tape (see page 17).

Tip
If the loops are still a bit soft, use rolled-up pieces of kitchen paper (paper towel) in between them to hold them in position until they are dry.

8 Using a No. 4 piping nozzle (tip), cut out small circles for the berries from thinly rolled out red flower paste and stick them on to the holly sprigs. Paint the stems on the holly sprigs using a fine paintbrush and brown colouring.

9 To make the pretty edging on the bottom tier 'ribbon', pipe small dots with soft-peak royal icing (see page 29 and 31). Pipe the first row of dots close to each other and touching the white band and then pipe another row touching the first, but missing a space after each one.

10 To make the bow, thinly roll out some red flower paste and cut strips about 12cm (4¾in) long and 2cm (¾in) wide. Make a loop and stick the two ends together with edible glue, squeezing them in slightly. Turn it on its side to dry slightly. Repeat until you have 15–20 loops.

11 Stick the loops together to form the bow before they are all dry using edible glue, then stick the bow on to the top of the cake.

Festive trees

I devised these quirky little Christmas trees to accompany the main cake. Fun to make and a heart-warming addition to a seasonal feast, they will also be much appreciated as homemade gifts for friends and family. Pack them in a clear box and tie a complementary-coloured ribbon around them to give them that extra wow factor.

Form the marzipan into cones to fit the tops of the cakes. Wrap thinly rolled-out white, red or green sugar paste around the trees, trimming any excess. Blend the join by rubbing your finger along the edge. Add a contrasting sugar paste strip around each base. Decorate with flower paste holly sprigs, as in the main cake, stars and circles, and piped dots of royal icing (see page 31).

You'll also need

Traditional fruit cake, baked in dariole moulds (see pages 40–41)

♦ Marzipan
♦ Green sugar paste
♦ Star cutter

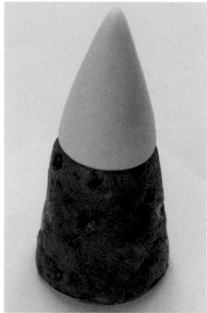

Candy cane cookies

I have used chocolate cookie dough here, but a gingerbread or another spiced cookie recipe would be equally good. These cookies would also work well as place settings – just tie ribbon around each candy cane threaded with a label inscribed with the person's name.

If you want to hang the cookies, carefully cut a small hole at the top with a tiny circle cutter as soon as soon as they come out of the oven when the dough is still soft. Cover the cookies with a piece of white sugar paste cut with the candy cane cookie dough cutter (see page 28). Thread the holes with narrow ribbon if hanging or tie around the cookies, if you like.

You'll also need

Chocolate-flavoured candy cane-shaped cookies, cut out using a cutter (see pages 26–27)
♦ Tiny circle cutter (optional)
♦ Narrow ribbon, for hanging or for tying around (optional)

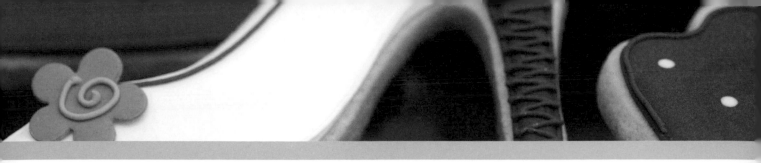

Dressing-up box

Everybody loves dressing up for a special occasion, so I thought it would be fun to extend that pleasure to create an haute couture collection of cakes and cookies that are likewise dressed to kill! I've focused on classic detailing and patterns for a timeless look of quality. The black and white monochrome scheme makes the whole effect striking and sophisticated, with a touch of colour added to soften the look.

Celebrate the theme

Carry on the monochromatic theme to create a dramatic table dressed in a crisp white linen tablecloth, embellished with a table runner made from gathered strips of white fabric topped with black ribbon and bows, to match the middle cake tier. Alternatively, translate the pin-tuck trimming on the bottom tier into a swag for the table edges and sides.

Pick up the pink of the corsage in the glassware and candles.

The napkins could be neatly pleated in the same way as the cake, and decorated with a real or fabric pink rose.

For something a little more fun and cutting edge, photocopy some fashion sketches or photos and use them to decorate the table instead.

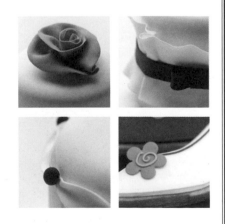

> "Everybody loves dressing up for a special occasion"

Couture confection

This dramatic design is straightforward to accomplish when tackled in easy stages, tier by tier. The flounce around the middle tier and the rose corsage that tops the cake involve the same technique of frilling the edges of flower paste strips using a ball tool.

Materials

One 10cm (4in), one 15.5cm (6in), slightly deeper than the other cakes, and one 20cm (8in) round white iced cake (see pages 34–41 and 12–15) ♦ One 28cm (11in) round black iced cake board (see page 16) ♦ Royal icing, 200g (7oz) (see page 29) ♦ White flower paste, 300g (10½oz) ♦ Edible glue ♦ Black flower paste, 25g (1oz) ♦ Food colourings: black, ruby and claret

Equipment

✧ 6 hollow dowels
✧ Large and small non-stick rolling pin
✧ Large non-stick board with non-slip mat
✧ Ruler
✧ Foam pad
✧ Ball tool
✧ Large, sharp knife
✧ Frill cutter
✧ Baking tray or old book
✧ Small piping (pastry) bag (see page 30)
✧ Piping nozzle (tip) No. 1 plain
✧ 1.5cm (⅝in) white and black polka dot ribbon
✧ Double-sided tape
✧ Black ceramic stand (optional)

1 Start by dowelling your bottom and middle tier (see pages 18–19). Stick the base tier on to the middle of your iced cake board with stiff royal icing. Allow to set slightly before adding your middle and then top tier.

2 To make the middle tier frills, roll out some white flower paste thinly with a large non-stick rolling pin on a non-stick board set over a non-slip mat. Cut out strips about 5cm (2in) wide and 15–20cm (6–8in) long. Starting with the outer frills, place them on your foam pad and frill one long edge by pressing down with your ball tool. Make sure that your tool is half on the flower paste and half off; you may need to carefully move it back and forth to create the frill.

5 Roll a long, narrow sausage of black flower paste, flatten with a rolling pin and then cut a straight line down each long edge so that they are parallel. Stick around the centre of the frills. For the bow, cut another strip of the black flower paste about 7cm (2¾in) long. Fold in the ends and wrap another short strip around the middle.

3 Gather the first strip for the top frill slightly to create a few pleats, then stick in place around the middle tier with edible glue. Repeat with the other strips to complete the frill, joining them together on the cake as you go and disguising the joins with a fold. Repeat this process for the outer bottom frill, leaving a 1–2cm (⅜–¾in) gap in between the two frills.

4 To create the inner frill, cut out a strip of white flower paste 5cm (2in) wide and long enough to fit around the cake, then frill as in Step 2, but this time lightly frill both long edges. Attach to the cake, gathering and pleating as in Step 3, but making it less ruffled.

6 For the top tier, roll out some white flower paste into a strip about 5cm (2in) wide and long enough to fit around the cake. Using your frill cutter, cut a scalloped edge down one long side and trim the other side with a large, sharp knife. Stick the strip around the base of the top tier with edible glue and cut away any excess paste to make a neat join at the back.

7 Tilt the cake very slightly using a baking tray or old book. Colour some royal icing with black colouring (see page 33). Use a No. 1 plain piping nozzle (tip) to pipe lines from the top of the scalloped edge, in between each scallop, to the cake base, squeezing a little extra icing out at the base (see page 31). Move the cake round as you work so that the line you are about to pipe is directly in front of you.

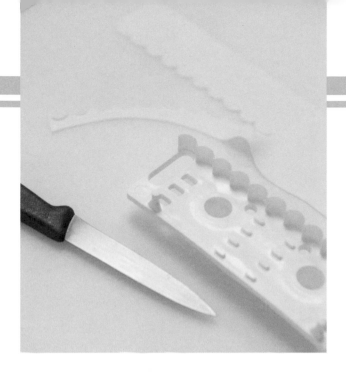

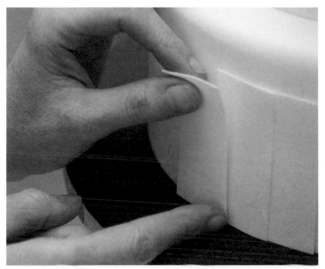

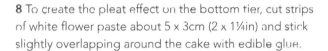

Tip

If the base of your middle tier looks a little messy, don't panic! Simply add a narrow white ribbon to cover any imperfections.

8 To create the pleat effect on the bottom tier, cut strips of white flower paste about 5 x 3cm (2 x 1¼in) and stick slightly overlapping around the cake with edible glue.

9 To create the pin-tuck ribbon effect, cut strips of white flower paste 1cm (⅜in) wide. Using a ruler, mark out even intervals to pinch the ribbon. Stick the pinched strips to the cake, resting on top of the pleats and joining together where the ribbon comes to a pinch. Roll tiny balls of black flower paste and attach to the pinched points.

10 To make the rose corsage, colour the remaining white flower paste with the ruby and claret colourings (see page 33). Roll out a strip about 5 x 20–25cm (2 x 8–10in). Frill one long edge as in Step 2 and then fold the straight edge over slightly.

11 Starting from one end, roll up the frilled strip, gathering as you go and creating a few pleats and folds to give the rose shape. When you get to the end, pinch the paste together at the base and cut off the stem so that it sits flat. Leave to dry before attaching it to your top tier with some royal icing.

12 Finish by attaching polka dot ribbon around your base board with double-sided tape (see page 17). Display the cake on a black ceramic cake stand if you have one or can get one.

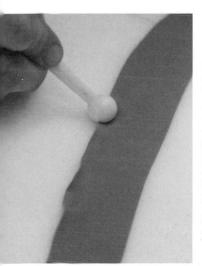

Designer delights

This selection of mini cakes features the three different designs used for each tier of the main cake, but reduced in scale. Present them on black doilies or a pure white ceramic stand to emphasize the monochromatic impact.

Simply follow the instructions for the main cake. For the ruffle cakes, use just a single strip frilled along both edges, and make a small rose corsage for the top of each striped cake in the same way as the large one.

Catwalk cookies

Here I've taken some of the main design elements used in the main cake – the black and white colour scheme, polka dots and pink corsage – to create a whole coordinating outfit. The cookies could be decorated in any colour combination to suit your preference or occasion, and are the perfect gift for any fashionista.

Pipe around the outlines of the baked cookies with a No. 1.5 plain piping nozzle (tip) and flood with either white or black-coloured royal icing using the No. 1 plain nozzle (tip) (see page 28). Then pipe on the details as shown in the photos, again using the No. 1 nozzle (tip). The corsage for the shoe is made by cutting a flower from ruby and claret-coloured flower paste using a small flower cutter, then decorated with a piped spiral of royal icing in the same colour.

You'll also need

Shoe, purse and dress-shaped cookies, cut out using cutters (see pages 26–27)
♦ Piping nozzle (tip) No. 1.5 plain
♦ Small flower cutter

Templates

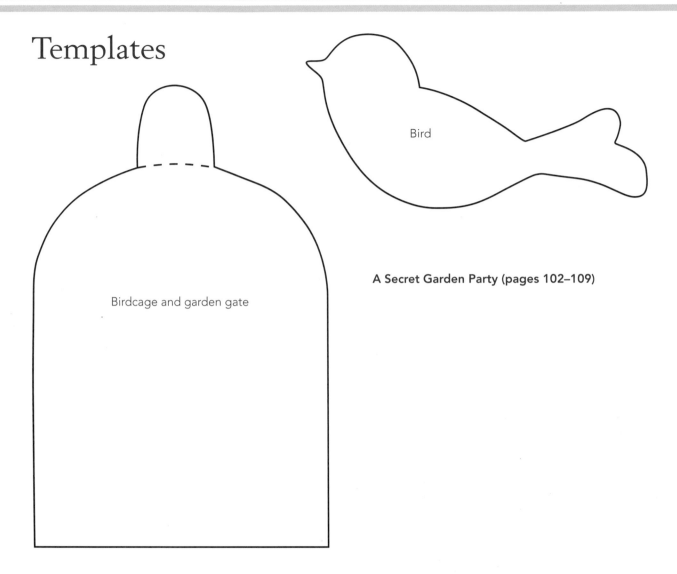

Bird

Birdcage and garden gate

A Secret Garden Party (pages 102–109)

Suppliers

Squire's Kitchen Shop
www.squires-shop.com
3 Waverley Lane, Farnham, Surrey,
GU9 8BB
☎0845 2255671

A Piece of Cake
www.apieceofcakethame.co.uk
18–20 Upper High Street, Thame,
Oxon OX9 3EX
☎01844 213428

Sugarshack
www.sugarshack.co.uk
☎020 8204 2994

Cakes 4 Fun
100 Lower Richmond Road, London,
SW15 1LN
☎020 8785 9039

Splat Cooking
www.splatcooking.net
☎0870 766 8290

US
Global Sugar Art
www.globalsugarart.com
625 Route 3, Unit C, Plattsburgh,
New York 12901
☎1-518-561-3039

Copper Gifts
www.coppergifts.com
☎1-620-421-0654

Acknowledgments

When I set up my own cake decorating business in 2008, I never dreamed that I would be writing my first book just a couple of years later, and I would like to thank everyone who has made all this possible.

Thanks to the fabulous team at David and Charles, especially the lovely Jennifer Fox-Proverbs for commissioning me to do this book and giving me such a great opportunity. I would also like to thank the extremely talented Sian Irvine and Joe Giacomet for their gorgeous photography and hard work.

Thank you to my parents who are always on hand for much-needed advice, and my two adorable children who love to help out at every occasion!. Finally, my biggest thank you goes to my wonderful husband Chris for his endearing support and patience.

About the author

After being inspired by making her own wedding cake in 2005, Zoe turned passion into profession and headed to London. There she worked with some of the UK's leading cake designers, and then decided to set up her own business, creating distinctive wedding and celebration cake designs that have drawn attention from both clients and the press.

Index